The
Principal
Chronicles

by David Garlick

Story Illustrations by Lindsay Chasten

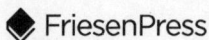

◆ FriesenPress

One Printers Way
Altona, MB R0G 0B0
Canada

www.friesenpress.com

ISBN
978-1-03-912574-2 (Hardcover)
978-1-03-912573-5 (Paperback)
978-1-03-912575-9 (eBook)

1. HUMOR, SCHOOL & EDUCATION

Distributed to the trade by The Ingram Book Company

September 7, 2021

Good Morning David,

I loved reading this, David. Part of my delay the last few days was that I had read it quickly at the cottage, started to scan it to remind myself of what I wanted to say, and ended up reading and savouring the whole thing all over again. You have captured life in our schools perfectly, filled with love and absurdity.

Please find the actual review below. Feel free to edit it as you wish.

"In this amazing book, David Garlick helps us journey back to our days in school. For both students and educators, the trip involves gentle laughter, goosebumps, laughing out loud and a few tears. It reminds us of the beauty of student music echoing along a marble hall, and the many dimensions of an educator's love of the work they do - a great read!"

Yours truly,

Mary Jean Gallagher

Note: Dr. Mary Jean Gallagher remains a mentor of mine, and a good friend. She was my vice-principal and principal 'a few years ago,' and then a superintendent and the director of my school board. Before I retired as a principal, Mary Jean had become a Deputy Minister of Education for Ontario. Her opinion has always mattered to me, and she has always been honest with me, so it was an act of bravery on my part to ask for her opinion of this book. I'm glad she liked it. Her most recent book is The Devil is in the Details: System Solutions for Equity, Excellence, and Student Well-Being, which she wrote with Dr. Michael Fullan.

Note 2: In spite of her permission, I didn't edit the review.

The Principal Chronicles: Mama Said There'd Be Days Like This

A Semi-Autobiographical, Pseudo-Non-Fictional Memoir Kind of Thing

Actually, she didn't. Mama didn't say there would be bad days, or interesting days, or whatever the title of the song by Luther Dixon and Willie Denson implies. It was my first boss, Elver Peruzzo, way back before the turn of the century, who said that the job would always be interesting—that if I was smart I'd never say, "Now I've seen it all," because I wouldn't have. Later that same day, or maybe as much as a week later, something new and different would happen. Something I'd have to share with a teacher, or friend, or another Principal, or, almost always, my wife.

I'm pretty good at telling stories. Often, at the end of an anecdote and a beer, my colleague or friend or wife would say, "You should write this stuff down! No one would believe this!"

That's what I'm doing. That's what this is.

I call it a semi-non-fictional memoir because some of the stories have been told so many times that I've changed them a bit from the reality of what actually probably happened years ago, and I've changed some names, and combined a few people into single characters, and I've forgotten a lot. I've since learned that this is called "creative non-fiction." No matter. It's still a pseudo-non-fictional memoir to me. Also, some of these pieces are works of complete fiction. I hope I've written them so that it's difficult to tell which are which.

But a kid did bring a coffee can full of snakes into the school.

The stories basically follow the arc of my career in education—from student to teacher, from teacher to department head, vice-principal, and principal—but they actually start before that and end after I retired. I'm a character in each of the pieces—usually the main character, hence "semi-autobiographical." But I wouldn't say I'm often the hero of the story. Sometimes I just happened to be there. And again, some of these things are completely made up.

For example, I did not, as an eight-year-old, convince a teacher to stop disciplining her students with a confiscated bolo bat.

There are, of course, several people I need to thank for this book. First, my wife, Linda, who has for more than half my life been my long-suffering first audience. It was to her that almost all these stories were told first. And then, sometimes for years, she had to listen to me tell them again and again (maybe that's why she told me to write them down...).

Of course, I must also thank my niece, Lindsay Chasten, who illustrated this book with some wonderful pictures.

Then there is Karen Demers, the leader of my book club, who, years ago, also told me to write these things down and suggested the title *The Principal Chronicles*.

The other first readers, or "beta readers," I'm told, were John Simpson, Graham White, Dave Dekindt, Elver Peruzzo, Ken Montgomery, Christine Vanderkooy, Leigh Vachon, Gordana Grmusa, Alice Aspinall, Kara Kristof and her father Steve, Amanda Sands, Sarah Preney, Anna Colledge, Annie Bondy, Deb Paetkau, Mike Thrasher, Jamie Benn and my sister-in-law, Darlene Chasten, who earns a special mention for editing the stories a bit and suggesting to me that some of them reminded her of Garrison Keillor and James Thurber. Dave Dekindt created the title of "The Keys to Being a Good Neighbour."

And of course, I need to thank the hundreds of teachers and thousands of students who have inspired and in some cases actually lived these stories.

So.

Let me tell you a story…

Author's Note to Educators

(My publisher has reminded me that you are my target audience.)

The stories which follow are all better experienced in person. Experienced, say, in my backyard on a summer's day after school has let out. Linda's prepared three or four salads, her famous Russian potato salad among them, and I've just barbecued a large platter of hamburgers and hot dogs, at least a couple of which are cooked just as you like them. There's an open cooler of soft drinks and beer on ice, and a pitcher of lemonade, cold and sweating in the sun. My suit and tie have been magically transformed into a Hawaiian shirt and shorts. You've brought a dessert.

I interrupt the conversations happening among the fifteen or so educators who are there, asking, "What's the funniest thing that happened to you this year? I'll go first."

Or maybe it's one of the monthly "non-obligatory, off-site staff meetings" at Rock Bottom Bar and Grill. You and I are picking at a plate of nachos. There are about thirty of us there. Maybe you had a rough day and need to talk with someone, but when you look across the table at me you see that, as usual, I'm smiling as I look around the room at the people we get to work with every day. "What made you decide to become a teacher in the first place?" you ask me.

Experienced in person.

But the reality is that those staff meetings and get-togethers are in the past, and you're reading this book instead. Maybe we never had the opportunity to actually work together. I hope, at least, that you're reading this in a comfortable spot at a comfortable time. Perhaps sitting on a beach in the summer, with your kids splashing in the lake. Or maybe you're at a cottage during March break. Maybe it's a Friday night and you're reading it in bed, intending for the book to help you relax after a long week.

I hope it does its job. I hope these stories make you smile and maybe laugh a little. I hope they make you laugh so hard, at least a couple times, that you wake up whoever is trying to sleep next to you.

I hope this book makes you ask yourself the same questions I asked myself and tried to answer by writing this.

Mostly, I hope you enjoy it.

Dave Garlick,
May 27, 2021

Table of Contents

Part One:
David as Student

On Becoming

I don't remember becoming a reader. I remember some moments along the path. I remember my mother taking me to Story Time at the Carnegie Library downtown. I remember "running away," often, to the John Richardson Library a few blocks from home and spending hours on the floor looking through the Beatrix Potter books by myself and never being interrupted by a staff member, or a concerned adult wondering where this child's parents were. At some point, the words became at least as important as the pictures, which were both charming and terrifying. If you don't believe me, take a look through *Peter Rabbit* and *Samuel Whiskers*.

I remember my mother being very disappointed that I didn't want to continue with Story Time at Carnegie, and also being disappointed that I'd forgotten to return a couple books that meant that now I had to pay a dime of my own money for the late fee. I also remember her warning me that maybe they wouldn't let me borrow books anymore, because I'd been so irresponsible. There may be a link between my wish to stop going to Story Time and having to pay the late fee. I couldn't run away to Carnegie because it was too far away from home and I was sure to get lost.

I remember always being able to read better than many of my peers in elementary school, reading ahead on my own, and getting into trouble for reading a different story than the rest of the class. Because of that, by the end of grade one, I'd lost the desire to demonstrate my reading ability by reading aloud. I did, though, like the books I'd thought the teacher had chosen for us.

By the time I was in grade two, I was reading the *Hardy Boys* series. This was because of a very beneficial sibling rivalry I had with my brother. Why should *he* be the only one to follow the adventures of Frank and Joe?

Any book was just about the best gift a person could get for me. That remains the case today.

I also don't remember when I became a person who was going to be a teacher, but I remember a few moments along that path as well. I was always good in English and History. Good in school, too. Never the *best* in most things, to be honest; there were always kids who were better than I was in Math and Science and French and far better than I was in Phys. Ed. I was always the kid with potential. "If he were to apply himself…" The truth was always that I didn't have to work very hard to be successful in grade school and high school. Being good enough was always good enough.

In grades eight and nine, I wanted to be a dentist. I remember telling my guidance counsellor this. This was largely because I thought they made a pretty good living and I wouldn't worry about being poor, and my mother would be proud of her dentist son. But I had an almost out-of-body experience at the dentist that year, saw myself with my hands in other people's mouths all day, and no longer wanted to be a dentist.

At about the same time, I'd read ahead in grade nine History and finished the textbook long before I was supposed to. I realized then that my History teacher, who was also my Phys. Ed. teacher, knew no more about British History than I did after I had read the textbook. If a question wasn't answered by the textbook, he didn't know the answer. Rather than just admit that, he told me to look it up myself and report back to the class. When I didn't—because I didn't *really* care when Whitsuntide was—I was given a detention. This taught me not to ask questions I knew he wouldn't know the answer to.

I also remember this History teacher getting really angry at somebody, not me, probably for being bored, and bringing his yardstick down hard on my desk to demonstrate this annoyance. I actually *had* been paying attention, so I wasn't shocked by the noise or his anger, which wasn't directed at me. I was shocked though, when his yardstick-smashing also resulted in the smashing of my red pen, which splattered ink on my sweater. I remember that he did not apologize. I also remember thinking, *I could do this better than you.* I was thirteen.

So maybe I do remember becoming a person who thought maybe he could be a teacher someday.

I had a wonderful English teacher that year: Donna Lanktree, now Donna Wishart.

It didn't hurt that I liked just about every book in the curriculum that year. It also didn't hurt that she gave us an assignment to write a play and then she thought mine was good enough to stage for the class. It was a comic piece about a hobo with a bad tooth. It also didn't hurt that I had a bit of a crush on her.

So, by the end of grade nine I was somebody who maybe might be a teacher someday, and if I *were* going to be a teacher, it would be a History teacher or an English teacher.

I pretty much sailed through the rest of high school, always doing well. In English and History, there were always kids with higher marks than I had, but I wasn't ever trying to get the highest marks. I remember, for example, a conversation with Miss Hastings, in which I acknowledged that Charles Dickens was a genius, but that as a fourteen-year-old, I'd rather read *2001, A Space Odyssey* than whatever thing by Dickens we were supposed to read that year. "I'll read that when I'm ready for it." She sighed and told me my mark would suffer, but couldn't really argue with my thinking.

I was competent in band class, and always enjoyed Music and Band. I loved being on stage and was in the school play every year. I made the tennis team. I did well, and looking back, all those things contributed to my desire to spend the next forty years in high school.

But there was a moment in grade twelve when I knew it was going to be my life's work, that it was no longer something that maybe might happen, but something that I'd work to actually *make* happen. I don't think that this is when I made the decision, but it's when I realized the decision had been made.

I'd been sick for a couple days and read a couple books during my absence from school. John Powers' *Do Black Patent Leather Shoes Really Reflect Up?*, which was far more funny and touching than "racy," as the title suggests, and Alexander Dumas' *The Count of Monte Cristo*. On my return to school, I had a conversation with the librarian, who was now Donna Lanktree, and casually mentioned that maybe our school library should get a copy of *Patent Leather Shoes*. I said this as I returned Monte Cristo to his place on the shelf. She said, "You think so? You know, David, I think you might be almost as well-read as I am." And then a week later, the book was part of the school's library collection.

Although I've reminded her of this conversation and the purchase a few times in the last forty-five years, I'm sure she doesn't remember the incident, because, for her, it was just something that she did, every day, as a good teacher. I don't know when I realized this. It was a defining moment in my life; those are rare, so I remember it as if it happened a week ago. Each thing I've mentioned above was a defining moment that feels like it happened a week ago.

Teachers create those moments all the time and may never realize it when they do.

Responsibility

Being a piece largely of non-fiction, if memory serves, to illustrate how old the author is and how he was raised in a more innocent time (as were we all).

My parents took it very well, I thought, when I announced to them that I was running away and planned to be a hobo. It was the summer of 1965, and if I was to escape the responsibilities of kindergarten, only a couple-few weeks away, I had to make a break for it now.

My mother had taken me to school to register me for fall classes at the time of year you were supposed to do that, which was probably February or early March, when I was still four. I misunderstood the purpose of the visit and was fairly certain my mother was going to leave me there. I found the building large, cold, and imposing. I was terrified. I remember lots of tears and having to be dragged to the office, which was on the second floor.

Neither my mother nor my father had taken me back to the building after this episode, fearing another such performance. Six or more months had gone by, and I knew that I was expected to start attending early in September, as I said, only a couple-few weeks away.

And so, I was running away.

There were no tears on my mother's part. Just calm acceptance. "If you're running away, you're going to need a good lunch," she said. "Would you like a cheese sandwich, or peanut butter and jam?"

"Cheese, please."

My father said that if I was to become a hobo, I'd need to have a stick and a large kerchief tied to the end, that would hold my lunch and my worldly possessions.

So we went downstairs to his workshop to find a suitable stick.

"I thought Mom would be more upset at me running away and wanting to be a hobo," I said to Dad.

"Well, everybody's got to be something," he answered. "At least you've got plans. A lot of kids your age don't yet."

So there were no tears from either of them. No imploring me to stay. No threatening to call the police. My mother was on the phone, talking with my grandmother, when Dad and I came back upstairs with the stick. "Yes. That's right, a hobo. No. I don't know when he'll be back." As I said earlier, I was quite surprised at how well they were all taking the news.

In addition to the cheese sandwich, on white bread and cut on the diagonal, the way I liked it, my mother packed me an apple and two chocolate chip cookies. My father wrapped them in a kerchief and tied this to the end of the stick. "You have to carry it over your shoulder," he said, demonstrating the technique. "All hobos do it that way. That's how other hobos'll recognize you as a real hobo and not just some kid."

My mother took a photograph of me, to remember me by. My father asked if he could walk me to the corner to see me on my way. "I guess," I said.

So my mother said good-bye to her second son and middle child and waved to me from the window as I walked away with my father.

When we reached the corner, my father asked me which way I was going to go. I told him that I didn't know, that I thought hobos just kind of drifted. I didn't have any firm plans.

"Well, if I were you, I'd go that way," he said, pointing in the direction of the elementary school I was escaping. "School's not in yet, so there won't be anyone there to try to talk you out of being a hobo. There's a playground behind the school, I think, with monkey bars and a merry-go-round. That'd be a good place to take a break and rest. Maybe eat your lunch."

That sounded like good advice.

"Be sure to write your Mom a letter to let us know how you're doing, okay? She'll worry otherwise."

"Okay."

And then I was off, running away in the direction of Prince of Wales Public School. It was three blocks away, a long walk for a five year old. When I got there, I was ready for a break. My father was right: when I walked behind the school, I saw there was a playground with monkey bars, a merry-go-round, and a sandpit. There were also two baseball diamonds and a soccer pitch. I sat on a wooden bench behind one of the baseball diamond's backstops and unwrapped my lunch. My father was also right in that there was no one there to talk me out of running away. There wasn't anybody.

Sitting there in the August daylight, eating a cheese sandwich cut on the diagonal, the building didn't look so scary. I finished my lunch, played for a bit on the monkey bars, and kicked some sand. I then walked up to the windows of one of the rooms on the main floor of the school. The teacher had already been setting it up for the coming school year and it looked pretty interesting. I walked all the way around the building, looking into every window I could.

The kindergarten room looked like fun. It was double-sized, with a stop light in the middle. There was a large wooden trunk that looked like maybe it was filled with toys. There were lots of pictures of animals on the walls and an open cupboard containing all different colours of construction paper. And there was a large shelf full of dozens of books.

The other classrooms I saw looked interesting but different than my kindergarten room. One thing I noticed was common to all the rooms: above the blackboard, there was an alphabet. Letters A to Z, both big and small. I knew all my letters already, and could sing their song by myself, with no help. I knew my numbers, too, and could count to twenty-five, I thought, without any help.

And then I remembered what my father had asked of me. I sighed. I put the hobo stick over my shoulder and walked back home.

"You're back!" my mother exclaimed. "Did you forget something? Or have you decided not to be a hobo?"

"Dad asked me to write you a letter to let you know how I was doing… I remembered that I don't know how to write yet. I thought maybe I should go to school until they taught me to write letters. I don't want you to worry about me."

You've Got to Eat a Pound of Dirt Before You Die

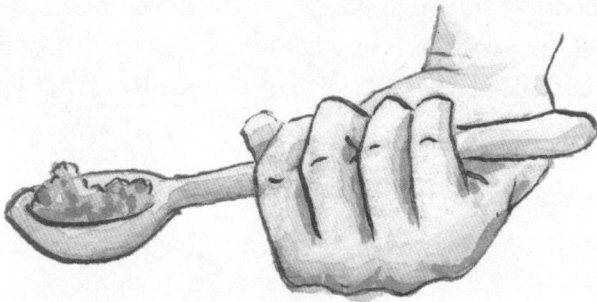

I was seven the first time I heard this expression; it was my father who said it to me. I think he must have been trying to console me when I'd failed in something at school or had gotten a lower mark than I'd expected. Or maybe it had something to do with Cub Scouts. I don't really remember. I *do* remember my dad saying it, though.

"You've got to eat a pound of dirt before you die."

It made no sense to me at the time. What did eating dirt have to do with anything? But rather than asking my father what he meant, I chose to be confused and then ask my friends about it later on.

And so, on a Saturday morning, in the school yard, Sidney Hartnick, Michael St. Amour, Bennie Talbot and I met to discuss the matter, sitting on the bench beside the baseball field.

"What do you suppose it means?" I asked.

"I dunno," Bennie answered.

"Search me," said Michael.

"Well…" said Sidney, who was six months older than I was, and therefore far more worldly in such matters, "what it *could* mean is that's how you die. Once you've eaten a pound of dirt—on accident of course—you die… That would explain why women live longer than men. They are far less likely to be eating dirt, even on accident…"

"No… Really?"

"You ever seen your mom eating dirt?"

"Well, no, but… really?"

"Do you think your dad just *says* stuff? Stuff that isn't real?"

I thought about this for a minute. My dad wasn't a liar. "Maybe it's just a 'spression. You know. Something people just *say*."

"So your dad *does* just say stuff!"

"Well… He also says, 'If dirt were dollars,' and that doesn't make any sense, either."

"I'd eat dirt for a dollar!" This from Michael St. Amour.

"NO YOU WOULDN'T!" "GET OUT!" "WOULD TOO!"

"How much?" Bennie calmly asked.

"WHAT?" Sidney, Michael and I asked at the same time.

"How much dirt would you eat for a dollar?" Bennie elaborated. "A dollar's a lot of money."

"I don't know… Not a *pound*! I mean, I don't want to die or anything…" Michael thought about it. "A tablespoon?"

"Make it two tablespoons. Like Bennie says, a dollar is a lot of money," negotiated Sidney.

The discussion had changed very quickly, as discussions often do when you're seven years old. We decided that we'd assemble the money by the next Saturday, and then Michael would eat two tablespoons of dirt for it.

"Just dirt though! No bugs or anything. No dog mess!"

A dollar *was* a lot of money. At that time, my weekly allowance was a dime, plus a dime for Cub Scout dues. Sidney, Bennie, and I could never raise that much money by ourselves in just a week. "We'll have to ask Rocky and Cabbage to partner with us."

No one ever knew Rocky and Cabbage's real names. We always called them Rocky and Cabbage.

And so, a week later, on a Saturday in May, we assembled again in the school yard: me, Sidney, Rocky and Cabbage, Bennie Talbot, and Michael St. Amour. Bennie also brought along his little brother, Jeffy, because he had to baby-sit that morning. Jeffy was four.

"Let's see the money!" said Michael.

Sidney added it up: two weeks allowance from me, twenty cents; a quarter from him; fifteen cents each from Rocky and Cabbage; and twenty cents from Bennie.

"That's ninety-five cents. Almost a dollar. So you don't have to eat the whole second tablespoon. You don't have to lick the spoon clean, okay?"

"Nothing from the squirt?" Michael asked, jerking a thumb at Jeffy, who had *his* thumb firmly shoved in his mouth.

"Got no money," he said around his thumb. "Too small for a 'lowance, Mom says."

"Michael," I said, "you don't *have* to do this, you know. What if Sidney's right, and you've almost already eaten a pound of dirt? You might drop dead right on the spot!"

"I'm not ascared! Give me the ninety-five cents!"

"Nope," Rocky said. "Fifty cents now and forty-five cents after you eat the second tablespoon!"

It hadn't rained in a few days, so Michael had to scrape the ground from behind the baseball diamond's backstop for the tablespoon of dirt. "At least this way, I know I'm not eating any bugs!"

And then he ate it.

He chewed and he chewed and he chewed and then finally he swallowed it down, making the grimace you'd expect from a seven-year-old boy eating a tablespoon of dirt.

We lost our minds.

We lost our minds the way five seven-year-olds and a four-year-old would. Cabbage ran around the baseball diamond shouting, "OH MY GOD OH MY GOD OH MY GOD!" Rocky and Bennie pretended they were going to throw up. I think Jeffy almost *did* throw up. Sidney and I laughed. "You actually ate a tablespoon of dirt!"

Michael just stood there with a silly grin on his face.

"Better'n Brussels sprouts!"

"Well, that was certainly worth fifteen cents!" said Cabbage, once he calmed down.

"One more for forty-five cents!" said Rocky.

And then Michael did it again, and he even licked the spoon!

We all agreed that we'd gotten good value for our money, clapping Michael on the back and continuing to pretend we were going to throw up. Michael was the hero of the day.

The *next* day, though, Michael and his older sister Kerry arrived at my door. Kerry was fifteen or sixteen and I had a bit of a crush on her. Michael held out his hand with two dimes in it.

"Mom says I've got to give the money back to you all and that what we did was really stupid and dangerous and stupid is as stupid does. So here's your twenty cents."

"How'd your Mom find out?" I asked, taking the money. "You didn't tell her, did you?"

"No! Somebody finked. Phone call. I'm guessing Jeffy couldn't keep his mouth shut."

"Only one of you lot with any sense!" said Kerry. "Only one of you to have two brain cells to rub together!"

Then they turned to leave. Kerry was clearly disgusted with all of us.

"Hey! Kerry?" I said, when they'd almost reached the sidewalk. "You look very nice this morning. Did your mom make you guys get dressed up to return the money?"

Michael was wearing a clip-on bow tie, and Kerry was wearing a skirt and blouse.

"Heathen! It's Sunday, numbskull! We just got back from church! I told my mother that the ninety-five cents should have gone in the collection plate, maybe help save a couple *deserving* kids in Africa, instead of just giving it back to you guys! But she said idiot-child here had to give it back and didn't trust him to do it by himself, so now I have to walk all over Hell's Half Acre with him to make sure he gives it all back! Now where do Rocky and Cabbage live? Idiot…". She cuffed Michael across the back of the head.

And then they were gone.

The phone rang about ten minutes later and although I only heard my mother's end of the conversation, I knew what it was all about, and I knew that I was in some trouble.

Mom sent me to my room after telling me that maybe I shouldn't *get* an allowance if that was the kind of thing I would spend it on, and maybe I shouldn't *have* any friends if that was the way I was going to treat them, and maybe I should just *think* about things until my father got home and see what *he* had to say about it.

My father came to my room about an hour after this.

"Your mom's pretty angry at you right now you know."

"Yeah…"

"She says no dessert for you tonight."

"I figured that…"

And then he smiled.

"Oh well. As they say, 'You've got to eat a pound of dirt before you die.'"

Enid Wakely and the Great Tornado of 1948

Before we get started, you need to know that this is a work of fiction. There was never a Miss Wakely, and even if she did exist, she wouldn't have taught me in grade three because I skipped grade three. I only had one mean teacher and she taught me in grade one. And just as importantly, there was no Great Tornado in Windsor in 1948 that killed seven people in Sandwich. There was a Great Tornado in Windsor in 1946, and it killed seventeen people. As a student and teacher of history, I thought you should know all that. Also, my brother Ken was never this mean. As a brother, I thought you should know that, too.

My brother and I had a complicated but understandable relationship when we were growing up. We're very good friends now. We travel together, golf together, go out to dinner once a month together—but it was different when we were kids. My brother is almost six years older than I am; I think there was a lot of resentment on his part when I came along and he was no longer an only child and had to share the affections of our parents. That resentment probably grew when he actually had to be *responsible* for me, watching his knucklehead brother when we were playing outside, keeping that same klutz of a brother from falling from the peach trees in the backyard (it somehow being his *fault* if I did). And then there was the *shame* of having to walk his kid brother to school when he was in grade six, for God's sake, and I was just in kindergarten.

For my part, there was also resentment. Although I looked up to my big brother the way any little brother does, Ken got to be in Scouts long before I did. He got to go camping, build model airplanes, own a wooden spinning top that whistled, put together puzzles with more than 100 pieces, ride a two wheeled bike, and—well there's just a lot of things you can do when you're six years older than your kid brother and an awful lot of times that kid brother has to hear, "Not yet, little man. You're just too young. Be patient."

None of this was either of our faults. And, like I said, eventually we outgrew the resentment. But for about twelve or thirteen years, I would not have wanted to be my parents dealing with either of us—separately, but especially, together. At times, "cats and dogs" described us. Or "oil and water." At the worst, we were "kindling and a lit match."

By 1966, I was in grade three in Miss Enid Wakely's class, and my brother had just graduated to high school. He no longer had to walk me to school and I had no interest in walking with him to my grade school. But as he had now completed the elementary school experience, he felt qualified to offer his advice and warnings about what I was probably going to experience. The fact that these warnings and advice were always given at night, as we lay awake in bed and away from our parents' ears, never occurred to me as suspect. How was I to know that Ken would delight in terrifying his little brother?

***

Miss Wakely was, to my mind, incredibly old. Older even than my grandmother. Easily the oldest person in our school. I don't now know that this was really the case, as anyone over thirty was impossibly old in my little mind, but I'd had a terrible crush on my grade two teacher, Miss Hunter, who had long blonde hair and wore the new *mini-skirt* and I'd heard that the other grade three teacher, Miss Hewson, was equally wonderful—but I ended up with Miss Wakely. In my defence, though, I should point out that Miss Wakely had taught both my parents, and she *looked* at least as old as my grandmother.

Miss Wakely had earned a reputation as being not only impossibly old, but also incredibly mean and nasty. This reputation was relayed to me by my brother, as I said, at night, in the days and weeks leading up to the start of school in September. Ken said that no one had ever seen her smile unless she was disciplining a student, or had just caught a kid out at something she could make fun of that student for. At some point in the late '40s or '50s, she'd confiscated some kid's bolo bat; at the start of each school year, she took it out of her desk drawer and threatened her class with it.

As things turned out, there was enough truth to what my brother said that I didn't doubt *anything* he'd said about her.

On the first day of school, Miss Wakely introduced herself to us by reaching into her desk drawer and pulling out her confiscated torture device. "This," she said, waving the bolo bat—which was missing the stapled elastic and rubber ball, but somehow, ominously, still had the staple, now rusty with age—"This awaits any *child* (she said the word as though she'd just swallowed a bug) who has the temerity to misbehave in my class." She paused for effect. "I prefer the bolo bat to the ruler or yardstick because it's less likely to break. And I prefer to administer my own discipline in the classroom as opposed to sending miscreants to the Principal's Office."

Our Principal, Mr. Barton, was a kindly old gentleman who'd driven me home in grade two after I fell from the jungle gym in the school yard and split my head open. I could not imagine Mr. Barton "administering discipline" in any fashion beyond a tear-inducing "I'm very disappointed in you, David" talk, but I knew that it wouldn't take very long for us to witness Miss Wakely employing the bolo bat.

For one thing, Miss Wakely supplied us with a *partial* list of the things that amounted to misbehaviour in her class: "Tardiness will not be accepted, whatever the reason. Talking out of turn or without first raising your hand and being recognized will also not be accepted." She went on to list seventy or eighty different things that would earn you painful whacks on the rump at the front of the class. To be honest, after "talking out of turn" was mentioned, I knew that I was a dead little boy and I stopped listening. Even Miss Hunter, who I loved, and who I'd fantasized also loved me (one day, I dreamed, I would push her out of the way of an oncoming vehicle on the street, sacrificing myself. She would visit me in the hospital as I recovered from my many injuries, kiss me *on the lips* in tearful thanks as I lay in bed with my arms and legs in casts, and then marry me when I recovered), even Miss Hunter had to speak to me, several times, about talking out of turn. In Miss Wakely's class I would be getting whacked daily.

"—And of course," Miss Wakely finished, "Anyone caught lying will earn the maximum number of swats with this little *device*! If there is one thing I can't, won't abide, it is being lied to." This was the way she introduced herself to us as a group.

When she went through the class register for the first time, she told us that when our names were called we were to raise our hand and call out "Here!" or "Present!" She left the choice up to us. Fear of the bolo-bat made everyone comply quickly and efficiently. No one called out, "President!" as Michael Grech had in grade one, whether out of cockiness or stupidity we weren't sure.

Upon reaching and calling out my name, I said, "Present, Ma'am," thinking the added politeness would stand me in good stead. She paused for effect and looked over her glasses at me.

"Garlick... I taught your brother, Kenneth, five years ago..." This was not a question. She was not looking for a response. She was just demonstrating her superior memory to the class. "He was an *able* student. Could have done better, if he'd *applied* himself. He's in high school now, I believe."

Now here's the thing. We were supposed to be impressed by these statements. She could remember students from *five years ago*! None of us even had any memories from five years ago (being three years old back then). And perhaps some in the class were impressed, but I wasn't.

Why not?

Well, first of all, Ken, as I said, had only just graduated to high school in June. He'd just left our grade school two months previously, having spent the preceding nine years there. Secondly, Garlick is a relatively unusual name. There weren't too many of us in the neighbourhood. I would *hope* an adult would remember the name. Thirdly, and most importantly, Enid Wakely was my neighbour. She lived in the same small apartment building as my family.

I didn't tell the class this. In the years since, I've wondered what would have happened if I had. "Yes, Ma'am. You taught my brother, who attended this school until two months ago, and who lives up the stairs from you, and has done so for the last nine years." Just matter-of-fact. Not sarcastic or expecting to get myself in trouble, but definitely sticking a pin in her bubble. But I didn't do that. I let her have her moment of superiority over a group of eight-year-olds, establishing on that first day in September just who was boss, who was in charge.

That night in bed—Ken and I had shared a room since our little sister was born—Ken said, "Yeah, she showed off the bolo-bat already, eh? I was hoping for your sake that maybe she'd wait a few days. That thing *hurts*! Some advice: when you're bent over, maybe tomorrow, with your head under the chalk ledge, be careful that your head doesn't snap up when she hits you. When you hit your head on the ledge, that hurts as much as the smack on your ass! Plus the kids always laugh when that happens. Doesn't matter who's getting whacked."

I nodded slowly. "Yeah. I'm dead. I'm bound to be the first one to get the bolo bat. She can't stand kids talking out in class, and I do that all the time. I can't help myself."

"You're probably right," he said (I wasn't). "She'll set an example tomorrow morning." (She did.) "The bolo bat is going to smack somebody for sure!" (It did.)

First thing next morning, Gord Thornton was the unlucky recipient of three whacks on the butt because he was five minutes late for class. And my brother had been right: when Miss Wakely whacked him the first time, bent over as he was at the front of the class, his head snapped up, hitting the chalk ledge, and creating a small cloud of chalk dust. We all laughed.

Later that week, we were treated to the other thing that Miss Wakely was famous for: the story of the Great

Tornado of 1948. Ken had told me about this as well. "This one thing is cool. She always tells the story of the Great Tornado of 1948. You can count on it."

At the beginning of each school year, the Principal was responsible to make sure that the student body was prepared in the eventuality of a tornado, fire, or a nuclear bomb, which seemed far more likely in 1966.

In the event of a fire, the fire alarm would ring. We were to get up and quietly walk out of the classroom, proceeding single file down the steps and out the girls' entrance of the school. We would gather as a class by the large maple tree, where Miss Wakely would take attendance.

We practised this one morning at the end of the first week of school. Mr. Barton rang the alarm and we did exactly as we'd been instructed. Afterwards, he congratulated us over the public address system: "We efficiently emptied the entire school in less than one minute and twenty seconds. If there had been a fire, I am confident that every staff member and student would have escaped alive!"

Our class applauded spontaneously. That seemed like something to applaud about. If we'd really been in danger, we would have all been saved...

This upset Miss Wakely; she hadn't told us we could applaud. But since it had been spontaneous among the whole class, there was no one to whack for it.

"One minute and twenty seconds might be acceptable to Mr. Barton. And he may be correct in assuming you'd all live, but in many previous drills we emptied the building in under a minute. One minute and twenty seconds, in my opinion, is nothing to celebrate. And it is *certainly* nothing to applaud for!"

Just before lunch that morning, Mr. Barton came back on the P.A. system to tell us that after lunch, we'd be having a tornado or nuclear bomb drill. Though these are very different scenarios, we were to respond to each in the same way: Mr. Barton would make an announcement, informing us either that a tornado was coming down the street, or a nuclear bomb was on the way. We were, as a class, to quietly get up and leave the classroom and go into the hallway, away from the big windows of our classroom. We would then line ourselves against the lockers, crouch down, one cheek pressed into the back of the person in front of us, eyes facing the lockers.

Again, Miss Wakely wasn't pleased. "I don't know why Mr. Barton told you there was going to be a drill. Whenever the school does something like this, I expect you all to act as though it's real. Your lives could depend upon it!"

"Miss Wakely, has there ever been a *real* tornado? I mean, I know there's never been a *real* nuclear bomb, but—"

"Of course there has! Jeremy, I hope you were not joking when you said that! A tornado is a deadly serious thing!"

Jeremy Buchanan was new to the school and new to the city, so I don't think he was joking; he just didn't know. As I said, in addition to the bolo bat, Miss Wakely was famous for one other thing, her story-telling of the Great Tornado of 1948.

"Please tell us, Miss Wakely." I said this in the most polite, most… servile voice I could.

"David Garlick. Was your hand up when you just spoke?"

I put my hand up. "I'm sorry, Miss Wakely. Jeremy's new to Windsor. I don't think there's any way he *could* know about it. Would you please tell us the story?"

"Well… we have a lot of math to get finished this morning, but we can spare a few minutes— but Mr. Garlick, it's not a *story*. It's an event. An anecdote. It happened."

"Yes, Ma'am."

"Let me see if I remember… It was April of 1948, just about eighteen years ago. I was teaching grade three then, in this very room. Spring had sprung, as they say, and I had noted that my daffodils were just about to bloom at home. Jenny, it's not polite to interrupt—what is it?"

"You had daffodils at your house?"

"That's hardly important to the anecdote, now is it? But yes, I had daffodils. And tulips. And crocuses. In any case, it was a Spring morning. The clouds were low in the sky and it was particularly windy that morning as I walked to school. I was glad I didn't have to use my umbrella, and also glad that my hair was in a babushka."

Gord Thornton laughed, "Ha! Babushka!"

"Mr. Thornton. May I ask what is so funny?"

"It's a funny word, ma'am. Babushka. It's just funny."

"Well I'm glad you find humour in this, Mr. Thornton, because, I assure you, there's nothing funny in the rest of this anecdote.

"As the day went on it got even windier. The Principal had to cancel recess because he was concerned that students would be injured outside. I remember I was teaching grammar. I looked out the window and saw it coming down the street, approximately a quarter of a mile from the school: a tornado!"

We gasped. Many of us knew what was coming, so it wasn't really a surprise. Still, a tornado!

"It was making its way up Wyandotte Street. I couldn't tell how big it was, but later the news reports said it was the largest in our history—Windsor's history, that is. Before it was spent, it would kill seven Windsorites."

Again, we gasped. Were they students? From our school?

"I didn't wait for an announcement or for permission. I gathered together my class, and we went into the hallway, just like we will this afternoon. When I saw that my class was in position, I ran from class to class alerting everyone. Soon, the entire school was in the hallways, and we formed large human caterpillars next to the lockers. "Be brave, children," I shouted, to make myself heard over the rushing noise of the killing wind. "Be brave, and keep your heads down!" It sounded like a freight train was coming right down the hall. The windows in our classroom and at the ends of the hallways broke. Some children screamed. It was over in just a few minutes, but it seemed an eternity."

"Did anyone die, Miss? Was anyone hurt?" This, from Jeremy.

"As I mentioned, yes, seven people lost their lives that day. A family in Sandwich. They lie buried in St. John's Churchyard."

"And at our school, Ma'am?"

"God be praised, no. There were not even any serious injuries. Though Jimmy Markham, one of our senior boys, *was* taken to hospital for observation. Later that day, the Principal came to my class, in this very room, to commend the students for their bravery and for following my instructions. And then he thanked me personally. He credited me with saving everyone in the school that day."

We applauded then. It seemed like the thing to do, and for the first time—maybe the only time that year—Miss Wakely smiled.

We talked about the story over lunch, which the students who didn't go home for lunch ate in the art room. "Eighteen years ago! Do you think she was just as old then?" "Well that's stupid! Obviously she was eighteen years younger!" "Yeah, but was she still *old*? Or do you think maybe she was young and pretty?" "Miss Wakely has always been old!" "Still, that was pretty brave of her, being an old lady and everything."

Our tornado drill went off without a hitch. We followed Miss Wakely's instructions, all pretending it was 1948 and she was about to save all our lives. It was the closest I came to liking her, and the last day I had any respect for her.

At the end of the day, Miss Wakely assigned us some math homework. I'd made it through one whole week without getting paddled, and one whole week without talking out of turn. I was so relieved that I forgot to bring home my math book. When I remembered after supper, I was too frightened to tell my parents.

I slept terribly that night. On Saturday, I confessed to my brother, who thought it was hilarious. His younger brother was going to get paddled by an old lady on Monday morning. "Ha! And you're the first kid to not do their homework this year! She'll want to make an example of you. She may even borrow the Principal's strap!" Ken was just having fun with me, but I was terrified. I'd heard about the strap. Three inches wide and a foot and a half long. Made from cow hide. And the rumour was that there was a metal blade running down the middle of it, to make it more stiff.

I dreamt of it all night long.

The next morning was Sunday. At church that morning, I confess to praying pretty hard for some kind of miracle that would keep me from the strap or the bolo bat the next day. I made the mistake of telling my brother that evening. "You prayed? To *God*? To not get the strap? Well, God will *probably* answer your prayer… but you know, little brother, sometimes he answers your prayers in unexpected ways. Maybe you won't get the strap, but it'll be the bolo bat."

"Nope. I prayed for that too."

"Oh…" And then he was quiet for a minute in the darkness. I know now that he was thinking as hard and as quickly as he could, but back then I thought he was just trying to *not* tell me the worst news. "You know, David, there are… other punishments…"

"What do you mean?"

"Well, the strap or the paddle are the most common, of course… but there's also *suspension*…"

Now, all these years later, I'm sure that Ken meant suspension as in keeping a student out of school for a day or more. For me, that would have been among the worst of penalties, and Ken knew that. But perhaps it was because suspension was a new word to me, as a school punishment, and because I'd been praying at church that morning, that I interpreted suspension as something akin to crucifixion.

"You mean she might suspend me from the ceiling? From ropes or something?"

Again, a short pause—

"Well, probably not with ropes... But yeah... something like that..."

If I was crying or whimpering in the darkness, I must have been doing it really quietly, because my brother was not *that* cruel. He would have said something like, "I'm just kiddin' ya. It'll probably be the bolo bat." So he probably thought I'd gone to sleep, and maybe I had, but my dreams that night were about being suspended from the ceiling of the classroom with ropes.

I ran to school early that Monday morning, and rather than wait outside, in one of the two straight lines, one for boys and one for girls, as I was supposed to, I snuck in, hoping to get my math book and maybe get my homework finished before school started. I was sitting at my desk looking for my math primer when Miss Wakely came in.

Did I confess? Throw myself on her mercy? No. I lied. I forget my exact lie, but it had to do with wanting to help another kid with their work, and when I couldn't say which student right away, she knew I was lying.

"Mister Garlick, you stay right where you are. Do not move a muscle, do you understand? I'm going to get the rest of our class, and when we come back, you'd better be exactly where you are right now."

The class came back about five minutes later. Five very long minutes. I'd say "the longest five minutes of my life," but those minutes were still to come.

After the national anthem and the Lord's Prayer, Miss Wakely called me to the front of the class.

"Now, Mr. Garlick, would you like to repeat the lie you told me this morning before class?"

"No Ma'am. I'm very sorry." I was also very scared and very near crying.

"Would you like to tell us the truth then?"

"Yes Ma'am. The truth is that—"

"I didn't ask you to tell us the truth. I only asked if you wanted to tell us. Now, raise your arms, Mr. Garlick."

"Pardon me, ma'am?"

"I said, raise your arms, Mr. Garlick. Like you're Jesus on the cross. He died for liars like you."

I was about to be suspended! From the ceiling! With ropes! Ken had been right!

At this point, I began wailing like I'd never wailed before. Wailing like maybe Miss Wakely had never experienced before. I had a complete meltdown.

"DON'T SUSPEND ME FROM THE CEILING WITH ROPES! I'LL NEVER LIE AGAIN!"

Miss Wakely's eyes opened wide. "WHAT ARE YOU SHOUTING ABOUT? BE QUIET, YOUNG MAN!" She tried to raise her voice above mine, but there's not much in this world that is louder than a terrified eight-year-old boy who doesn't want to be suspended from the ceiling with ropes.

"SHE'S GOING TO SUSPEND ME FROM THE CEILING WITH ROPES AND LEAVE ME THERE! DON'T SUSPEND ME FROM THE CEILING WITH ROPES! PLEASE DON'T SUSPEND ME FROM THE CEILING WITH ROPES!"

Looking back, as an adult and educator, I know that what happened next was because I'd succeeded in scaring the old lady. My shouting and wailing would soon attract the attention of every adult within earshot. What could so terrify a *child* on a Monday *morning,* and so close to the beginning of the day? If I kept it up, soon the teacher from next door would have looked in, and then the Principal and his secretary. And Miss Wakely and I would have to explain what was going on, and where would I have gotten the idea that I was about to be, in effect, crucified? Because that is what I know, as a more than sixty-year-old man, *know* she was going to do to me. She was going to put a couple books in each of my hands and make me stand there until I cried or until I dropped the books, and *then* she would have paddled me. And even in 1966, that was not something that you did to a child.

"MR. GARLICK! BE QUIET AND SIT DOWN! AND DON'T EVER LIE TO ME AGAIN!"

But as an eight-year-old boy, I believed that what had just happened was a miracle, brought about through the power of prayer.

I sat down, and after about ten minutes I was back to normal. Miss Wakely didn't call on me for the remainder of the day, maybe for the whole week, which was fine by me. And to the best of my recollection, we never, as a class, saw the bolo bat again. Student discipline would be referred to the Principal from that day on.

Miss Wakely never even mentioned the incident to me again. I endured a few days of gentle ribbing from my class-mates for my over-the-top performance, but they all had to acknowledge that I'd escaped any real punishment for not doing my homework, sneaking into the school and class-room, and lying to Miss Wakely. They all had to admit, as well, that being suspended from the ceiling was something Miss Wakely was capable of doing to us. And they were all grateful to me that the bolo bat seemed to have disappeared.

After a few days, no one mentioned the incident again.

My father was a firefighter and spent forty-eight con-secutive hours away from home each week. So he wasn't at home that evening to ask me how my day was at school. He also hadn't been home the Friday evening I'd told Mom about the Great Tornado of 1948; he got home Tuesday morning, after I'd left for school.

That evening, over dinner, he asked, "So, Dave, did anything exciting happen at school this past week?" I chose, for the second time—because I hadn't told my mother the previous evening either—not to mention my almost crucifixion. I never did mention it to them. I didn't want them to think of their son as a liar.

"Miss Wakely told us all about the Great Tornado of 1948 and how it killed a whole family in Sandwich."

"Ah yes… I remember that. It was very sad. Do you remember, Hon? They'd just gotten home from church, and the tornado tore off their roof."

"Church?" I asked.

"Yes. They were a religious family, and they'd all gone to church that morning. Because of that our minister said they'd died in a state of grace and went straight to heaven."

"But why would they go to church on a school day?"

"It wasn't a school day. The tornado of 1948 happened on a Sunday."

An Odd Apology: Addendum to Enid Wakely and the Great Tornado of 1948

My brother is a sort of villain in "Enid Wakely and the Great Tornado of 1948." I have him set me up to be terrified of the old, mean teacher with the bolo bat and help me to envision a completely unreasonable punishment. I mean, really—suspended from the ceiling by ropes? But the thing is, to an eight-year-old, such a punishment *is* reasonable—which makes the story both funny and believable. It's what makes the story work.

What *isn't* believable, at least to me, is the way the author makes my brother behave. If you know my brother and me, you know that part of the story is fiction. Ken was, and is, a good big brother.

This is the kind of brother he was:

Just like in the story, Ken and I shared a bedroom. We shared a bedroom for many years. At some point, it became a pretty good thing for both of us. I can't tell you exactly when, being the younger of the two of us, but at some point, we became friends. That was definitely not the case when we started out sharing a room. I would have been, what, four? Meaning Ken would have been ten.

Ken had been an only child for six years until I came along. And then a few years after that, he had to share his room with me. This was not easy. For one thing, I have never been a good sleeper. I walked in my sleep. I talked in my sleep. It took me hours to fall asleep. For a time, I was convinced that I *didn't* sleep. And, for a time, I was afraid of the dark.

In the same way it is reasonable for an eight-year-old to believe he could be suspended from the classroom ceiling by ropes, it is entirely reasonable for a four year old to know that there are monsters under the bed or murderers outside the window. And that a night light next to the bed would somehow keep them all at bay.

Now Ken, at ten, knew there were no monsters or murderers. He also knew that a night light would keep him awake, but so would a four year old whimpering in the darkness. So this is how he cured me of my fear of the dark.

One night, as we lay in our twin beds, with the big light out, but the night light next to my bed burning bright:

"Hey... Dave?"

"Yeah?"

"You know I used to be afraid of the dark too, right?"

"Yeah?"

"Yeah... Want me to show you how to stop being afraid?"

"Is this a trick?"

"Nope."

"Okay."

"Turn off the night light, but leave your hand on the switch in case it doesn't work, okay?"

"'kay."

"Turn it off when I get to five. One… Two… Three … Four… Five."

I shut off the light. Complete darkness.

"Now just listen."

"For what?"

"Just listen, okay?"

And then—after a few more seconds—with me straining my ears in the dark—he farted. A real ripper. And I started to laugh. And he started to laugh. We laughed until our father called out from the front room. "Hey! You kids be quiet in there!"

We both did out best to suppress the laughter, but it was difficult. It took a while. As soon as I'd calmed down though—

"Hey Dave… Listen…" He whispered.

I started to laugh again.

"Don't make me come in there!" warned our Dad.

All this time the night light remained off

"We'd better stop laughing, eh?"

If there is one thing that is more fun to a four year old than laughing with your big brother in the darkness, it's trying *not* to laugh with your big brother in the darkness. And nothing keeps the monsters and murderers at bay more effectively than trying not to laugh with your big brother in the darkness.

If Anyone Here Present...

In the eight years of my grade school career, from kindergarten to grade eight (I skipped grade three), two of my teachers got married during the school year: my grade four teacher and my first French teacher. Miss Johnson became Mrs. Simpson, and Mademoiselle Turner became Madame Lennon.

I won't write much about Mademoiselle Turner becoming Madame Lennon because it hurt too much at the time. I had a terrible crush on Mademoiselle Turner and secretly hoped that she'd marry me after I finished grade school. I was too young to see *The Graduate*, but even if I had, I don't think she'd have been very impressed by an eleven-year-old interrupting the service by pounding on the glass in the church like Dustin Hoffman did for Katherine Ross. Mademoiselle Turner *did* look a bit like Ms. Ross, though. And everyone was disappointed to hear that, no, she didn't think her fiancé was related to John Lennon of the Beatles. So I wouldn't have gone to the wedding, even if I was invited, but I wasn't in any case.

This raises a point I'll deal with quickly. This was before the title "Ms." existed.

I mean no disrespect, and would have gladly called both these women "Ms." if the term existed and if they'd asked me to. This was a time before Ms. but after teachers were required to resign if they were female and had the audacity to fall in love and get married. So, in general, teachers getting married was a pretty positive thing, unless you were an eleven-year-old who wanted to marry your late-twentysomething French teacher.

Now, Miss Johnson was another matter. I really liked her. We all did, I think. I didn't take a poll or anything, but all my friends agreed that Miss Johnson was a fine teacher, pretty cool for an older person, and definitely deserving of happiness in her private, out-of-school life. By grade four, we all knew that our teachers had lives outside of school. We'd seen many of them in the grocery store, for example. And after asking our parents about it, we were assured that they also ate food. Our teachers went to the movies too. Miss Johnson may even have seen *The Graduate*, but she never talked about it with us.

So, I liked Miss Johnson, but I didn't have a crush on her. I was eight, I think, or maybe nine, depending on when she got married. I don't recall the exact month she was married… What I *do* remember is that she invited us, her class, to the ceremony. This was amazing! I'd never been to a real wedding, having only seen a few on TV and seen pictures in the paper. I ran home to tell my mother after school. She expressed incredulity: "She didn't actually invite you."

"Yes she did! She invited all of us! She said, 'It would be really nice if some of you could be there. It would make the day extra special,' she said!"

So my mother called the school and spoke to Miss Johnson. Yes, she had asked us to attend the service, if we'd like. My mother called a few of the other parents. Some thought it a beautiful gesture. Some, my mother included, said it wasn't the smartest thing to do. Both views, as things turned out, were correct.

Matthew Parker and I decided that we'd go together. The church Miss Johnson was getting married in was downtown, and by grade four, we both knew how to get there. We went by this church on the bus on the way to the movies.

"You know," Matt said to me on the way home after school, "There's a moment in the service when Miss Johnson kisses the guy who becomes her husband."

"Yeah, I know. We don't have to watch that though. Can you imagine kissing anyone in public like that? I mean everyone's *looking* at you!"

"Bet you want to kiss Linda like that!" said Matthew.

"Shut up!" I responded.

That's how old we were.

A few moments later, Matthew said, "There's another part where the minister says something like, 'If anyone objects to these two guys getting married you better say something, like right now.'"

"Yeah, I heard that too."

"And if anyone says anything then they can't get married that day."

"No?" This was news to me.

"No. The thing gets called off. Everyone has to go home. And then I guess the minister has to interview the person who objected.

"That'd be terrible, eh?"

"Yeah". Again, a few moments went by. " I was thinking maybe I'd object." Matt said, matter of factly.

"What?"

"Yeah. I'm serious! What do we know about this guy? Have you even met him?"

"Well, no, but—"

"I've heard that people do crazy things when they're in love. What if Miss Johnson's crazy in love with this guy and he's a murderer or something?"

"Matt, you wouldn't!"

"Nah. I'm just funnin' ya." He punched me in the shoulder, proving, I guess, that he'd been joking.

And then we were in front of my house, and saying good-bye, and I was saying I'd see him tomorrow morning and reminding him he needed to wear a tie.

"I heard it's not that kind of a church and we can wear a sweater if we want."

"My parents are making me wear a tie."

"Mine too. Just funnin' you again."

I didn't tell my mother about the conversation I'd had with Matt. I worried that she'd overreact, call Matt's mother, and get Matt in trouble, and then maybe not let us go to the wedding at all.

But that night, I had terrible dreams in which Miss Johnson's fiancé actually *was* a murderer. In one dream, Miss Johnson couldn't see it at first, and then told me she *wanted* to marry a murderer—that she'd change him, and if she couldn't change him, then she'd be a murderer, too, and they'd murder people together! And then, in my next dream, her fiancé wore a black cowboy hat in the church so we all knew he was evil, and he looked kind of like Dracula, and Miss Johnson kept saying, "Isn't he the cutest thing?" just like Charlie Brown's little sister says about Linus in *Peanuts*.

They were terrible dreams. But then I woke up and it was Saturday morning and I had to get ready for the wedding, which was, I think, really early in the afternoon. Matt and I knew it would take about an hour to walk to the church. We'd told our parents we were going to take the bus, so they were going to give us bus fare which we'd save and then use to buy some french fries at our favourite dime store, Kresge's. If we left early enough, we could have the french fries before the service.

So we left in plenty of time and walked to Kresge's before going to the church. Along the way, I told Matt about my dreams.

"You know," he said, "I've heard that some people's dreams predict the future!"

"Yeah, I heard that too…"

"Maybe your dreams are those kind of dreams."

"Matt…"

"I'm serious! Maybe your dream is telling you that Miss Johnson *is* marrying a murderer and she's only marrying him because she's crazy in love! And it's gonna make *her* into a murderer and—"

"Shut up!"

"I'm just funnin' ya."

That's how old we were.

And then we were talking about baseball, probably, or Kresge's and their french fries and what did we think the gravy was made from.

And then we were at the lunch counter in Kresge's eating our french fries. Matt opted for the gravy, which I never did, because Matt always told me what he thought the gravy was really made from. I'll leave that to your imaginations. Suffice it to say, we were eight-year-old boys.

And then we were sitting near the back of the church. An usher had asked us if we were friends of the bride or groom and I said, "Neither. Miss Johnson's our teacher," and they seated us near the back of the church. There were six of us from Miss Johnson's class in that row, and Matt and I were the only boys. Linda told me I looked very handsome in my dad's tie, the back of which was stuffed into my shirt because I was still about eight years from being big enough to actually wear an adult's tie. Boy, did that make me blush.

Linda whispered, "I'll bet Mr. Simpson is *really* handsome."

Melissa added, "Yes. Dreamy!"

Matt said, "Dave thinks he's probably a murderer and he looks like Bela Lugosi."

"I do not!"

"Dave says he going to object when the minister asks us if we have any objections!"

"I did not!"

All of this was in a whisper, of course, except for my "I did not!" I think most of the church heard that.

"I'm just funnin' ya . . . *I'm* going to be the one to object!"

"You are not!" we all whispered.

And then the service started. Miss Johnson looked beautiful as she walked by us. I was pleased to see that Mr. Simpson was not wearing a black cowboy hat, and looked nothing like Bela Lugosi.

The service was longer than I thought it would be, and the church hotter. Some people had air conditioning in their homes at this time, but no churches did.

Matt leaned over towards me. "I don't feel so hot."

"Well I do!" I whispered back. "It must be like a thousand degrees in here!"

"No—I don't feel so hot! Do you think they'd let me go to the bathroom or something? I think maybe it was the gravy."

"Stop goofin' around, Matt!"

An old woman on the Simpson side of the church turned around and put her finger to her lips, shushing us.

And then the minister was saying, "If anyone here present—"

And Matt stood up.

I whispered, "Matt! No!"

In my memory, which I admit can be faulty, the entire church turned around to look at Matt, but I don't know how that could have happened because I only whispered. "Announce" is the wrong word for what Matt did, but I don't know the correct word. I'm certain most of the congregation heard him say, "I'm sorry. I have to go to the bathroom!" —and then he ran to the back of the church, hoping that that was where the bathroom was.

Linda gave me a look of sympathy, quietly conveying the message, "I'm sorry he's your friend." At least she wasn't blaming me. And at least the service wasn't called off. No one objected. Miss Johnson became Mrs. Simpson. And I watched her kiss her new husband.

On the way out of the church, Mrs. Simpson, my *teacher*, kissed me on the cheek and thanked me for coming. "Is Matt okay?" she asked.

"I think he ate something that didn't agree with him."

Linda asked me if her father could give me a ride home with them. I politely declined. "Someone should go home with Matt." I said. "And I don't think he should be getting into anyone's car right now."

"Man, was I sick! Barely made it outside! Wanna see?"

That's how old we were.

More than fifty years later, I still remember the new Mrs. Simpson kissing me on the cheek. It was a beautiful gesture to invite us all. And as my mother thought, it maybe wasn't the smartest thing to do.

That time I killed Christopher Prynn

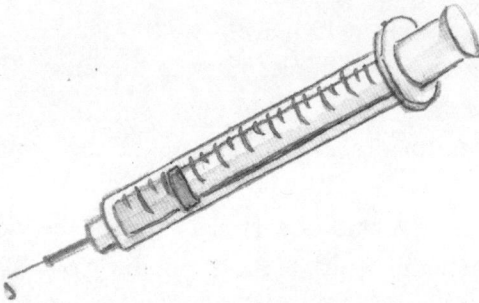

I am not a violent sort of person. I can't remember ever hitting anyone in anger. Except for the couple of occasions when I was beaten up by the neighbourhood bully, Wayne, I've never even really been in a fight.

Once, as an adult, I was punched in the face. I was a manager at McDonald's. It was late at night. We were closed, doing the nightly clean-up and money-tallying before we ended our shift, when there was a knock on the door. The three people outside said it was an emergency. I opened the door to talk with them and it turned out that the emergency was that they were a bit drunk and needed some hamburgers but we were closed.

"Come on, man! Just give us a couple burgers, man!"

"I'm sorry," I said, "but we're closed. We've shut off the grills."

It was then that one of them punched me in the face. I was more surprised than hurt. He went to punch me again, but I grabbed his fist in my hand. "Is that supposed to make us more likely to open up for you? We're closed!"

"Sorry man…" His friends couldn't see his face, but I saw what looked like big fear in his eyes. It gave me a neat kind of feeling, to be honest.

"It's okay. Try Burger King up the street. They might still be open, I don't know."

"Hey, thanks man! Sorry about the punch in the face…"

That's the kind of person I am. Not the violent sort. And yet, I refer back to the title of this piece, "That time I killed Christopher Prynn."

I'm not violent, but I *am* afraid of needles. I used to be *really* afraid. It was a major deal for me a couple-few years back when I took myself to the hospital for a tetanus shot after slicing my leg open on some rusty eavestroughing. I looked down at my bleeding thigh and thought, "How long has it been since my last tetanus shot?" My memory for such things is pretty good. "About fifteen years…" I answered myself. I cleaned up the wound, dressed it with a clean gauze pad, and took myself to the hospital. "Better a shot than lockjaw," I reasoned.

I was quite proud of myself.

When I went for the fifty-year-old's colonoscopy, the worry for me wasn't anything to do with the snake going up my hoop, or the prospect of being told I had cancer, or the day of close proximity to the toilet. For me, the worry was the needle that would sedate me before the procedure. Again, I was quite proud of myself just for going.

Most recently, I was actually excited at the prospect of getting the COVID-19 vaccine and quite happily went to get it as soon as I was able to.

But in all of those cases, I was an adult in my fifties and early sixties. I've come to realize that my dread has slowly morphed from dread to abject fear, to a simple kind of phobia, to a dislike. I dislike needles now. I'll get them when I have to, will avoid them if at all possible, but will eventually go to have blood work done for my annual physical, for example. And if I'm doing my bit to end a global pandemic, I'll actually enjoy them.

When I was fourteen, the situation was quite different. I was *terrified* of needles. I'd spent more than a month in the hospital at age five as a very sick young boy, getting needles and blood transfusions on what seemed like a daily basis. Until I was well into my thirties, my father always introduced me with, "This is my son David. He pretty near died."

Anyway, I didn't die, but I did develop a terrible fear of needles.

I don't know if it's still the case, but back when I was in grade ten, everyone in grade ten had to get their booster shots for measles, mumps and rubella, or they couldn't stay in school. If you were a Jehovah's Witness, or Amish, I think you could get a pass, but nobody else could, and I was neither of those.

So I had to get my booster shot. At school. In public. Along with everyone else in grade ten.

Now, many of my friends weren't in grade ten. They were in grade eleven. I don't know why that was the case, but it was. They were all older than I was, and well through the ordeal of the booster shot.

They all knew how frightened I was of shots, and thought that was a very funny thing. They also knew that, in certain cases, I was pretty gullible. I would believe anything I was told about the booster shot.

"It's nothing!" said Carter Reid. "Nothing to worry about at all! You don't even feel it! They use a gun, you know…"

"What? What do you mean, they use a gun?"

"Yeah. A gun," said Roland Matthews. "They hold it up to your shoulder, pull the trigger, and the needle *shoots* into your arm."

My jaw dropped.

"But you've got to be careful, because if you move or anything, the needle can get lodged in the bone or shoot straight through your shoulder. In one side and out the other…" Carter added.

Now I should mention that Carter and Roland were the children of ministers. Two different ministers, but both children of ministers, Anglican and United. They wouldn't lie, right?

I walked away even more terrified than I was before, if that was possible. I'm certain that after I left them, they both doubled over in laughter. In fact, I have a completely impossible memory of them laughing at me, I'm so certain of that.

So anyway, on the day of the booster shot, my mother made me go to school. Back when I was seven years old, she'd taken me to the doctor's for a tetanus shot and had to catch me as I tried to race from the examining room. I'd asked the doctor if the needle was going to be in my shoulder and, as a joke, he said, "No, Dave. I'm going to stick it in your ear!"

I threw my hands over both ears, leapt off the examining table, and raced for the door. My mother caught me just as I saw daylight. I still remember the look of shock in the other patients' eyes as I screamed in my mother's arms.

So anyway, my mother made me go to school that day in grade ten.

We were called out of class and told to go the typing room, converted for the day into an infirmary.

We got into a line leading to the room of the booster shot.

As luck would have it, just behind me in line was Katie Lester. None of us knew it at the time, but Katie would grow up to become a Doctor of Nursing. When we were in grade ten, she was just a really cute kid I had a bit of a crush for, and really nice.

"Hey Katie? Listen, could you do me a favour? I'm a bit terrified right now. I don't want the needle to shoot through my arm or anything, so—

"Shoot through your arm?"

"Yeah. When they pull the trigger. Anyway, look, I'm going to close my eyes when we get through the door, okay? So if you would do me a favour and kind of just sort of, I don't know, walk me to the table or chair or whatever …"

"Sure, Dave. Not a problem."

I'd had a bit of a crush on her, as I said, but when she said that and didn't laugh, and didn't ask me if I was crazy or a chicken, well, I fell a bit in love with her then.

We got through the door. I closed my eyes. Katie walked me to a table and sat me down.

"This is my friend, Dave Garlick. He's a little bit scared right now. Would it be okay if I stayed with him until you're finished? I'll have my shot next, if that's okay."

Now I was completely in love. My eyes were firmly closed and I began to ramble—

"Uhhh. Listen. Nurse? Would it be better for this to be in my left arm or my right? I'm left handed you know. Uhhh. Don't tell me when you're going to do it, okay? I'll try not to move when you pull the trigger but I was wondering, uhhh, how many people have the needle lodge in their shoulder bone? And uhhh, (I felt the cool of the alcohol soaked cotton ball) how many have the needle shoot right through—"

"We're done."

"What?"

"We're done. You can go."

I opened my eyes. I looked down at my shoulder. There was the tiniest drop of blood.

"There wouldn't even be that tiny drop of blood if you hadn't been shaking so much!" said the nurse, who

I noticed then was really quite young, and really quite pretty. She was smiling at me.

Now I began giggling in nervous relief and said, "So I can go?"

"Unless you'd like another shot..."

I jumped off the table and sort of drunkenly stumbled towards the door. I've never been one for false bravado, so I didn't say anything stupid to the kids who were still in line. I didn't think to thank Katie, though, and for that I still feel some shame and regret. I didn't end up thanking her until our class reunion some twenty-eight years later.

Anyway, I left the room and began walking back to class. Before I could get there, I ran into Carter, Roland, Rory Jeffries, and Christopher Prynn. For some reason, they were gathered in the hallway.

"Hey Dave! How was the shot?" I forget which of them asked me. It was probably Carter or Roland. Rory wouldn't have cared, and if it was Christopher, he would have been asking out of interest or concern. He was a nice kid. So, either Roland or Carter added, "Yeah. How was the *gun*?"

By this time, the four of them had circled me, waiting to hear my answer.

"Aww. It was nothing! I was expecting a doctor to come up and *shoot* me in the arm—"

When I said, "*shoot* me in the arm" I made a motion with my arm as though I'd been shot in the shoulder. I wasn't paying any attention to where any of the four of them were standing around me, or how close we were to the lockers. The back of my right hand caught Christopher Prynn under his chin, snapping his head back and into the lockers. It made roughly the same amount of noise as a locker does when you slam it shut, so it didn't attract any attention from the classes that were going on.

Christopher's eyes rolled back in his head and he slid slowly to the terrazzo floor.

"Jesus Christ, Dave! You killed him!"

Christopher was gone. His eyes were now closed, and a bit of spittle appeared at the corner of his mouth. I dropped to my knees next to him.

"Chris! Christopher!" I slapped him lightly across the face. "Christopher! Wake up!"

For about ten seconds, I thought I *had* killed him. Ten seconds is a long time to think you've killed anybody.

Eventually, though, he came back to us. *A propos* of nothing, the first thing he said upon returning to the living wasn't to tell us about a tunnel of light or a feeling of great peace; instead, he looked me in the eye, slowly coming back to consciousness, and said, "It must have been the stuffed tomatoes…"

Being the fourteen and fifteen-year-old kids that we were, none of us thought that perhaps Christopher had sustained a concussion, and that, maybe with a group of nurses in the building, we should have him looked at. He'd just been dead for ten seconds or so. No big deal. We helped him to his feet, dusted him off, and we all went back to class. Or at least, I know I did.

Quite the day: for about ten seconds, I was a murderer. And I fell in love.

Quite the day.

Useless and Useful Questions

When we were in grade ten, Eric Pruellers made it a practice to ask a useless question at the beginning of English class every day. He told me in September that this was his plan and goal. He thought it would be a fun way to start the morning off and that he didn't think that Miss Marston would mind. "In fact, I'm kind of hoping she enjoys it."

By the third week in September, we, as a class, had begun to look forward to these questions, and, as Eric hoped, so did Miss Marston.

The bell would ring, we'd stand, the national anthem would play, we'd sit back down, we'd listen to the morning announcements, and then Eric's hand would shoot up.

"Yes, Eric?" Miss Marston acknowledged.

"Miss? Except for the rhyme, is there any reason for the expression 'Drunk as a skunk?'" I mean, animals don't drink at all. Are skunks supposed to be drunker than other animals?"

Or,

"Miss? Who *were* Tom, Dick and Harry? And why shouldn't my sister go out with them?"

Or,

"Miss? Why is the short form for the plural of Mister, M-E-S-S-R-S? I mean, shouldn't the short form for Misters be Mrs.? It would probably be confused for Mrs., but what is Messrs even short for?"

The questions were never rude. Eric never really expected an answer, and the questions were never anything that we'd heard before. There was no, "Miss? Why *is* the sky blue?" or "Miss? Could God make a stone so heavy that even he couldn't lift it?" But there was a "Miss? If God made a stone so heavy he couldn't lift it, would he use marble, do you think? Or maybe a rougher type stone, something that would give him better grip?"

As an aside, Eric had almost perfect attendance that year, and we all looked forward to these questions each day. Once, in November, Eric was away with a cold. He called me the night before to ask me if I would read the question for him. "Don't try and imitate me or anything. Just put up your hand and say, 'Miss? Eric's sorry he can't be here today, but he was wondering'—and then ask the question, okay?" That day turned out to be pretty important to Eric. At the end of the class, Ruth Madoff came up to me and said, "Eric trusted you to read the question for him, so you must be good friends. Would you do me a favour? Please tell Eric that I think he's really funny, and kind of cute, and that I'll say yes if he asks me to the dance next week. I'd tell him myself, but… anyway, please tell him." Eric and Ruth celebrated their fortieth wedding anniversary this year, and I was their best man.

Every day that year, from September through to February, Eric started the day by asking his "useless" question. And then we'd laugh, or groan, or maybe just smile. But one day, late in February, after the national anthem and morning announcements, Eric put up his hand and asked, "Miss? Why do some people have to be so mean?"

Miss Marston's smile disappeared and she asked almost immediately, "Eric, is someone being mean to you?"

"No... Not me. I'm funny, so no one picks on me. And not Dave, either. I mean, he's really good in English and reads a ton, and we all respect that. And Graham and William and Kathy, well, they're all super smart. And other kids, they're good at music or sports or drama, or maybe they're just really good-looking. But there are some of us who aren't any of those things... yet. But we're only fourteen or fifteen years old. Why would anyone be mean to anyone else when we all have so much time left, and none of us know how things will turn out? It doesn't make any sense. Does it?"

I'd never seen any teacher respond like this before, but Miss Marston teared up, wiped her eyes, and walked over to Eric's desk. "Stand up please, Mr. Pruellers."

Eric stood, a bit confused, but then Miss Marston hugged him and said, "In twenty years of teaching, that is the most beautiful thing I've ever heard. Thank you. I'm proud to know you, Eric."

And then we all applauded.

We had eight classes a day back then, and I think I was in four of them with Eric, plus lunch. He was quiet throughout Math class, which was right after English, but at lunch he had a group of five or six seniors come up to him and say, "Pruellers? Marston told us what you said this morning. You know something? You're all right, kid. You're all right."

And then, during French, which was at the end of the day, our class was interrupted by the vice-principal, who asked if he could speak to Eric in the hall for a minute. It was really about five minutes, but when Eric came back into class, he had a big smile on his face.

"Everything all right, Eric?" asked Mr. Vandervaart.

"Yes, Sir. He just wanted to thank me. Miss Marston told him what I said this morning, and apparently she told all the teachers in the staff room at lunch. He said he's had a few kids come up to him today to apologize for their behaviour this year and promise not to bully anyone any more. He knows that it probably won't last, but that, at least for today, it was refreshing. He thought it might be embarrassing to just come right into class and tell me, but he asked if he could call home and tell my parents they've raised a great young man! Geesh! Sorry! I mean Zut! Alors!"

On the way home that afternoon, I asked Eric who he was referring to when he asked why people were so mean sometimes. We'd both been bullied by Jeremy Woodbridge in grade nine, but that was over, and he was still trying to be especially nice to us.

"Oh, no one in particular. I was watching something on TV last night about a bully and his victims. It was supposed to be funny, I guess, but it got me thinking. I thought about Jeremy and what you had to do to get him to stop last year. But none of us knows where we're going to end up or what we'll turn out to be. Jeremy could have been bullying a future prime minister for all he knows, or maybe just the kid who'll grow up to be the cop that gets to pull him over for speeding. We're all just *kids* …"

The next morning, like clockwork, Eric's hand shot up.

"Yes, Eric?"

"Miss? I forgot to thank you for what you said yesterday, and for the hug. That had to be the best day of my life so far."

"Well, you're welcome Eric. And thank *you*, again."

"Miss?"

"Yes Eric?"

"So last night I dismantled an old shelf in the basement and I was wondering, why is it no one ever mantles anything?"

W. O. Mitchell's Lumber

When it came to my schooling, I was a lucky man. Having been a teacher and principal for more than thirty years, I saw and heard a lot of horror stories when it came to kids' education and their choices: parents who threatened to disown their children over potential educational pathways, demands being placed on children to become doctors or lawyers. "No son of *mine* is going into the arts!" "Just find yourself a good man and settle down. Give us grandchildren before we die."

I never had to deal with such things. And I don't know why.

My parents never questioned my desire to study History and English. Never once was there an attempt to talk me out of it. No "What are you ever going to do with a degree in *History*?" And when I told them I wanted to go to Queen's University for teachers' college, they took some of Dad's vacation time that spring to look for an apartment for me in Kingston while I finished up my undergrad degree.

They were always supportive of any decision I made.

Part of this, I think, is that my father, a product of the Depression, quit school in grade ten and went to work for the next fifty years— first in a succession of part time jobs, and then as a firefighter starting just before I was born. Those first twelve years after quitting school could not have been easy for him and I think he was happy his children wanted to stay in school as long as we did.

But we never talked about it. He never asked me how things were going at school, or what I was learning, or what I was going to do with it. Those things were outside of his experience, and it always seemed—*seemed*—that he just didn't get it.

I remember, though, coming home one evening in late September or early October, incredibly excited. I was in my first year of university, studying both History and English. I'd been walking through the halls of one of the larger buildings on campus when I came to a set of fire doors. I opened the door on the right and realized that there was someone behind me. I turned and held the door to let that person, whoever it might be, precede me through the door. I've always done that, taught to do so by my father.

My jaw dropped when I saw who I was holding the door for: W.O. Mitchell! One of Canada's greatest living writers! I'd heard that he was the university's writer-in-residence, but I never expected to actually *see* him!

"Thanks very much, young man! Have a nice day!"

And then he was gone. Before I'd had the chance to close my mouth or say anything to him, even, "You're welcome, Sir." I'd been spoken to by W.O. Mitchell! No one else in my History class later that afternoon seemed very impressed by my story. Some of the kids I spoke to didn't even know who he was.

When I got home that evening, I told my parents all about it. "He wrote *Who Has Seen the Wind*! A classic! I had to read it in grade twelve! Everybody has to read it!

And he thanked *me* for holding the door for him! He's giving a writers' tutorial next week and I'm going to go!"

"He's pretty good, eh?" said my father.

"One of the best!"

My father is not a reader. Well, that's not entirely true. He's read just about everything that Zane Grey has written, novels about America's Wild West, but that's it. Maybe once every five or six years, he'll find something he wants to read, but I've never been able to figure out how he chooses it. For example, the autobiography of Dave Dravecky, a baseball player who continued to play after losing one of his arms. It *was* a good book, but I have no idea how he found it, or why he thought he might want to read it, when he reads so little. My mother reads a lot, but when I was in university, it was mostly Harlequin romance novels—maybe two or three a week.

I didn't think they ever really *got* university, or what I was doing there. They were both just happy that I was happy.

Anyway, that's where our conversation ended. My father and my mother were both more impressed than my fellow History students had been. Even though they hadn't heard of Mitchell either, they believed me when I said how good a writer he was, and also nice enough to thank me for holding the door for him.

I attended Mr. Mitchell's workshop the next week. He taught me how to "collect the lumber" that would become my short stories and to use my own experiences in what I wrote. And things went back to normal with my parents. As long as I was happy and passing my classes, they had no concerns and expressed no interest in what happened on a day to day basis. We didn't talk about Mr. Mitchell again.

I did all right that semester. Didn't tear the place up or "eat it up with a spoon," like I would later tell certain students they would every year when I was their teacher, but I did okay. And I was very happy when we got to Christmas break and I could stop being concerned about British History and American History and the survey course of English Literature I'd been taking for four months, at least for a couple weeks.

I forget most of what happened that break. It was a long time ago, and one Christmas is pretty much like any other Christmas. But I do remember my father handing me one of my gifts that year. It was clearly a book, and it was also clear that my father had wrapped it, because he wrapped gifts better than my mother.

I tore it open to find *Since Daisy Creek* by W.O. Mitchell.

"Thanks! This is great!"

"Open it up." My dad smiled.

I opened the cover of the book. There on the title page, in bold cursive penned with India ink, was written,

"Merry Christmas, David! W.O. Mitchell."

"Holy Cow! It's signed! And to me!"

"He seems like a really nice man," said my father. "I have no idea how you find your way around that university! I must have gotten lost seven or eight ways to Sunday before I found his office! But he was happy to sign when I told him how much you liked *Who Has Seen the Wind*. Merry Christmas, son."

Maybe they *did* get university. And what I was doing there.

Part Two:
David as Teacher

Never Leave the Class Alone

As odd as it will sound when you read it, this story is true. I've no idea why Herbert did what he did.

This is how old I am: I went to teachers' college at a time when film projectors were a "thing," so we had to learn how to thread a film projector and properly choose and attach the take-up reel. It was a time long before VCRs, DVDs, and Blu-Rays. And this meant that actually watching a film in class was always a treat, even if you didn't particularly like the movie. And depending on which teacher was trying to show the movie, it could also be an adventure.

That's how old I am.

I forget why or how Herbert Longmoore was chosen by our Audio-Visual professor that morning to *act* as the teacher of a grade five class, and we, as a group, were chosen to *act* as a class of grade fives, but it meant that Herbert had to thread the film projector, attach the correct take-up reel, introduce the movie, and then show it to us.

It also meant that we, a group of teacher candidates, were to act the way a group of eleven-year-olds would in the same situation.

The film was *Paddle to the Sea*. That's how old I am. You can look it up or watch it on YouTube. Actually, *Paddle to the Sea* is even older than my teachers' college days. Our grade school watched this movie in the gymnasium in 1967, the year after it was nominated for an Academy Award, and the year our country turned 100 years old.

Anyway, Herbert threaded the film projector and attached an appropriate take-up reel. Then, leaving the lights on for the time being, he introduced the film to us.

"Class? This is an award winning National Film Board movie that follows a boy's hand-carved and hand-painted canoe, which he names *Paddle to the Sea*, from the moment it's placed in the headwaters above Lake Superior all the way to the Ocean—"

"Which ocean?" One of us, now pretending to be a student in grade five, asked.

"Pardon?"

"Which ocean? The Atlantic or the Pacific?"

"Could be the Indian Ocean…" I said. Again, we were supposed to be a class of eleven-year-olds.

"Garlick, you're a knucklehead."

"Hah! Teacher called you a knucklehead!" I think Herbert was getting tired of the pretend eleven year olds.

"Shut up!" I said. I wasn't getting tired of it. This was fun.

"The Atlantic. It's the Atlantic." Herbert said, ending our erudite discussion.

Herbert started the movie and asked Brenda Foster to turn the lights out. She only flickered them a couple times before actually turning them off and sitting down.

And then we sat back to enjoy the movie, which most of us remembered from grade school and actually enjoyed when we first saw it. And Herbert Longmoore did what *some* teachers would have done back then, I think. He made sure the movie projector was actually working correctly, and then he left the room for a cigarette. Like I said at the start, I have no idea why he would do this.

What were we going to do? We were supposed to be a class of grade five students watching a movie in class, and it was one we actually enjoyed. As I said, this was before the era of VCRs, so watching movies in class was still an uncommon thing. And watching a film you enjoyed was even more uncommon.

Someone threw a ball of paper across the room.

"Knock it off! I want to watch this!" "Me too!"

And so we behaved.

But as it happened, Herbert Longmoore, who had chosen an appropriate take-up reel, hadn't attached it correctly, and just as *Paddle to the Sea* was going over the Niagara Falls, the take-up reel fell off the back arm of the projector, hit the floor, made a big noise, and shot to the back wall. *Paddle to the Sea* continued to fall as film began to collect on the floor.

A few of us got up to see what we could do to help the situation.

Our professor laughed and said, "What would a class of eleven-year-olds do?"

We sat back down to watch *Paddle to the Sea* make it to the St. Lawrence Seaway before Herbert Longmoore returned.

"Jesus Christ! Why didn't anyone do anything?" Herbert ran towards the projector.

"Teacher swore!"

"Shhh! I forget how this ends."

The room went dark as Herbert turned the machine off.

"Uhhh, Brenda, would you turn the lights back on, please?"

The vast majority of *Paddle to the Sea* lay in a jumbled mess at the back of the room and at the bottom of the desk the projector sat on, like so much celluloid yarn or cooked pasta. Herbert Longmoore looked like he was going to cry.

"You may as well turn the movie back on, Herbert. It's going to have to run all the way through before we can put it back on the reel anyway." This was Tom Malloy.

"We?" This was me. The knucklehead.

We watched the rest of the movie, probably only five more minutes, in which the once brightly painted but now weathered and water worn canoe is rescued from the Atlantic Ocean and then thrown back in to continue its trip, maybe to Africa or England—at least that's how I remember it—and Herbert quietly seethed.

The film ended and we applauded; the bell went and we all got up to leave. All except for Herbert Longmoore. And our professor returned to the front of the room.

"Have a nice day, class. See you next week. I'm glad you all learned something today. Be sure to snap the take-up reel in place before you begin. Listen for, and feel, the snap—or be sure the toggle is pushed down—and of course, never, ever, leave a class of grade five students alone."

Elvis Presley and My Second Teaching Report

The week before my second round of practice teaching in teachers' college in Ottawa, a short train trip away from my university in Kingston, the music teacher was fired at the school where I was to be teaching. He had been caught in a rather compromising situation with one of his students in a practice room.

This was the talk of the staff and student body the week I arrived. *Everyone* was talking about it.

My associate teacher, the man who would be responsible for me while I was at his school, sat me down before the first class on the first day and told me all about what had happened.

"So, Dave, even though you're, what—twenty-three years old?—and even though some of the students you'll be teaching are eighteen or nineteen years old and there is no way you'll be teaching them again after you leave us, it would be a *really* stupid thing to get caught with one of them, okay?"

Lesson taught. Lesson learned.

I had a very successful teaching round. The kids were great; I did very well and received an excellent report from the Associate.

But on the very last day I was there, a Friday afternoon, one of the students came up to me at the back of the class where I was talking with the associate. I had yet to receive my report.

"Excuse me, Sir?" She was talking to me. "A few of us are going out this evening to Jimmy's Piano Lounge, and we're wondering if you'd like to join us. If you don't know where it is, I'd be happy to drive you."

The young woman "asking me out" was in grade thirteen and nineteen years old. She had long, wavy blonde hair and was strikingly beautiful. I'd never been asked out by a woman before. And she was strikingly beautiful.

And I was sitting next to my associate teacher, who hadn't given me my teaching report yet. And the student was strikingly beautiful.

"Uhmmm… Thank you very much, but I'm going out to dinner with a few other student teachers this evening (I wasn't). I really appreciate the offer!"

"Oh. Okay. Have a nice time, Sir. You were a really good teacher."

The associate never said a thing to me about this "incident." He gave me my report and told me I'd done very well—that he hoped there would be teaching positions at the school in the coming year, and he'd put in a good word for me. To this day, I wonder whether he'd set up the incident and had asked the young woman to come back and say what she did.

In any case, when I got back to the place I was staying in Ottawa, I called my mother to tell her about the report and what had happened with the beautiful young woman. She thought it was hilarious. Laughing, she said, "Oh, David. There will be other young women. Don't you worry." I still felt pretty sorry for myself at the missed opportunity.

Now here I need to digress. Stay with me.

By this time, three of my grandparents were dead. All three had died with some form of dementia. My last remaining grandparent was my mother's mother, who was, I think, seventy-six years old in 1982, when this story happens. Dementia has an element of heredity about it, so I always watched her with concern. So long as she remained "with it," there was a fair chance that I would not, necessarily, develop dementia.

Anyway, two days later, on Sunday morning, when I was back in my apartment in Kingston and still feeling a bit sorry for myself, I received a phone call from my grandmother. This was the only time I remember Grandmother ever calling me.

"Hi David. This is your grandma. How are you doing?"

"Fine, Grandma! Thanks for calling! How are you?"

"Oh, y'know." She often said that. It was part of her speech pattern. Most sentences either started or finished with it. It didn't mean anything, it was just a sentence-starter or finisher.

"Your mother called me last night to tell me how proud she was of you about your teaching report."

"Oh! That's nice. I had an excellent time at that school!"

"Yes. And she told me all about that girl who asked you out."

"Oh… Yes…"

"Y'know… Elvis Presley had all kinds of girls asking him out in the 1950s and '60s."

"Yes…" This is the reason I digressed to tell you about my three other grandparents dealing with dementia, and why I was always watching my last remaining grandparent.

"When he sang at concerts, those girls just swooned! They threw hotel keys at him, some fainted, and some even threw their underwear at him. Y'know."

"Yes. I've heard that…" At this point, I was thinking I'd have to call my mother to break the news that *her* mother was beginning to "lose it."

"And Elvis Presley made millions and millions of dollars off of those girls."

The conversation would have to start, "I'm sorry Mom, I just got off the phone with Grandma and she wasn't making any sense. Maybe you should go over and check on her…"

"Well, y'know, I just called to tell you that if you'd gone out with that girl, you wouldn't have made any money off of her at all!"

We laughed and laughed.

I did call my mother about an hour later, but only to tell her that Grandma was pretty cool for a seventy-six-year-old, and to thank her for telling Grandma that she was proud of me.

Two Teachers

After teachers' college, I spent a few years as an occasional teacher, a supply teacher. This wasn't by choice. There were just no full-time teacher positions in History or English when I returned to Windsor after my time at Queen's University. Looking back, this was probably a good thing. I used this time to hone my craft. I had the opportunity to watch dozens and dozens of very fine teachers who were all willing to offer me advice and help a young teacher out. Stepping into a classroom with no preparation, and sometimes no work left for me, helped me develop the skill I still call "tap dancing." The years I spent as a supply teacher made me a better classroom teacher.

There were several teachers I really enjoyed teaching for as an occasional teacher. Marcia Higginbottom was one of them. It's not that she was a particularly good teacher, or had such wonderful rapport with her students that it made it easier for a supply teacher coming in. She was neither hated nor loved. It's not even fair to say that she was respected, but the students didn't actively disrespect her, either. She was just a teacher that the kids had. If, after they completed their four or five years of high school you were to ask them to list their teachers, like as not, she would be one of the ones forgotten. Not a *bad* teacher, just not a stand out.

And I certainly didn't like her near-addiction to the photocopier. Virtually every lesson relied on that machine. Once I understood that, I made sure to arrive at school at least a half-hour before classes started. It would take at least that long to photocopy the materials necessary for the day's lessons. The other teachers were sympathetic when they saw I was in for her, and they'd let me cut in line.

By the way: always, *always*, when Marcia used the photocopier, she'd end up jamming it. But always. And she could never figure out how to clear the jam.

Never.

"Ummm… Could someone help me in here? It seems the machine is acting up again."

Now, granted, the machine did not only jam for Marcia. But it *always* jammed for Marcia.

Because of that, I became very proficient at clearing jams, loading the machine with paper, fanning the pieces in the humid spring and summer so they wouldn't stick together, printing documents on both sides of the paper, etc. Because of Marcia, I became a photocopying expert, something valued by many other members of staff.

But this expertise was gained at the expense of a lot of patience. "No problem, Marcia, happy to help." So it was definitely not a reason for me to enjoy teaching for her.

Why did I enjoy teaching for her, then?

Marcia Higginbottom left detailed, minute-by-minute instructions for each of her classes throughout the day. Minute by minute. Written on the board, if she knew in advance she was going to be away. National Anthem: 8:50–8:52; Announcements: 8:52–8:57. It drove her crazy if the morning announcements went beyond the five minutes she'd allotted for them each day. She'd furiously erase the end time and adjust the remainder before she could even begin to take attendance (scheduled for 8:58–9:00) and so on throughout the day. Class discussions were limited to five minutes, no matter what was being discussed or how involved the class was in that discussion. Marcia had an internal clock that told her exactly when it was time to switch gears from one topic to another. Sometimes she would consult the clock on the wall behind her, but that was almost always just to confirm that her internal clock was working well.

You'd think that kids would find this noteworthy—either really interesting or super annoying—but most just seemed to accept it. It's just what happened for seventy-five minutes of their day, every day.

Unless I was there.

I was a little confused by this schedule the first time I saw it. I asked each class and was told, "That's the way Ms. Higginbottom does it, Sir."

"To the minute?"

"Yes, Sir. All the time."

"Well, she did change it when we had the fire drill…"

"Yeah, well she had to, didn't she?"

"But apart from then…"

So the first time I looked at that schedule with an actual class, I did something unheard of in Ms. Higginbottom's class. I asked them not to tell on me because I didn't want to get in trouble, and then I erased all the times.

"I'll make you a deal. When we ALL get all this stuff done, class is over. I mean, you can't leave or anything, I like having a job, but when we're done, we're done and the rest of the time is yours. Deal?"

You wouldn't think it would make that much difference, but it was just audacious enough to generate interest. How much free time could they earn, they wanted to know? Or, if we were having a really good class discussion they'd make me a deal. "Tell you what, Sir. Let's finish up the rest of the work, and if there's time, can we come back to this? It's really interesting and deserves more time."

Ms. Higginbottom was pretty sick that year, so I was in for her a lot. She had regular treatments, I'm guessing for cancer or diabetes or kidney failure, so she knew in advance what days she'd be away and usually have the schedules written on the board for me.

On the days I was in for someone else, and Marcia was there she always made a point of commending me for getting the work she had assigned done. "Some supply teachers don't even try, you know."

"And some classroom teachers don't leave any work at all, so I really appreciate what you do as well."

She never mentioned my particular approach, so I'm guessing, all these years later, that the students never mentioned it to her. At least, she never complained about me to the principal.

So far as I know, only one teacher ever complained about me to a principal: Mr. William Procter, who ended up being, if not an actual friend, certainly a friendly and supportive colleague. The day after the first day I was in for him, he marched down to the office from his third floor classroom to register a formal complaint and demand that I never teach his classes again. I clearly had no control over a classroom and he did not, in future, want to put any of his students at risk!

What had or hadn't I done to demonstrate this danger-ous lack of control?

The vice-principal, who didn't really know me at this time, expressed the appropriate concern, but to her credit did not promise to black-ball me without getting all the particulars first.

"Did he deal with the work you left behind for him?"

"Yes."

"Did he leave you a note about the day and what was accomplished?"

"Yes."

"Did he leave you a list of any problems he had with any of the students?"

"That's the problem! He claimed to have had a great day! And that he had no problems whatever! That's how I know that he had no control!"

"William, I don't understand. He got all the work done that you wanted, left you a letter to that effect, and said that you had great students! What more can you ask for? What did he do that was so bad?"

The important fact that I've left out to this point, admittedly on purpose, is that Mr. Procter suffered from obsessive compulsive disorder. That's my diagnosis, anyway. Classroom blinds were raised or lowered to be exactly aligned. The date appeared in blue chalk in the top right corner of the blackboard, every day. Desks were in perfect rows of eight, and the students in those desks were always seated alphabetically.

As a sort of parlour trick, not unlike Marcia Higginbottom's internal clock, I encouraged the students to sit wherever they liked after I took attendance. Then, when the students told me to, I'd go up and down the rows telling the students their names. Generally, I was very good at this, and if I made a mistake or completely forgot, I'd claim a girl I didn't know was Audrey Hepburn or Elizabeth Taylor. Boys were Paul Newman or Robert Redford. They loved it. Apparently, to Mr. Procter, this was risky behaviour.

And the kids, knowing that I had no way of knowing, and probably wouldn't have cared much in any case, put their numbered Merriam-Webster dictionaries back *in the wrong desks!*

To be fair, this could have led a person like William Procter to an embolism.

The VP took down the complaint about me and told Mr. Procter she would be reporting the incident to the correct authority, who turned out to be the principal.

After school, with the office door shut, she told him all about what I'd done.

They laughed and laughed.

Years later, she told me the story. By that time, I was a vice-principal and she was a superintendent. Fifteen years had passed and so had William Procter—as it happened, from an embolism, but about ten years after he had retired.

I don't know if he ever made the connection between the supply teacher he'd complained about and the young teacher who was hired to teach in the classroom next to him. He never mentioned it to me, and we always got along very well. He always stopped by for a few minutes on Friday mornings when my class had doughnuts, and when he retired, he offered me all his class notes. "I won't have any use for them. They belong with a good young teacher."

He was talking about me.

Mental Illness

Now that I've retired, one of my new duties or responsibilities is to be a caregiver to my parents. They're both medically fragile, Dad on oxygen twenty-four hours a day, Mom dealing with Parkinson's and osteoporosis. But they're still living in their own home and getting by.

I don't want these duties to sound overly onerous; I appreciate how lucky I am to still have them both as I myself start to look at old age not too far away on the horizon. I drive my parents to their medical appointments, help them navigate tax season, and occasionally I'll shop for them, picking up their groceries. I also helped them install their new "Help, I've Fallen and I Can't Get Up" alert system. My brother and sister and their spouses all help out as well and my parents' neighbours cut the lawn and shovel the snow.

So it's not too bad.

Recently, I was with my father in a clinic's waiting room, I forget what for. There weren't too many patients waiting that day, and my father had figured out that we were only going to have to wait for two or three more people until it was our turn.

Often, my father has issues with his "social filter," due mostly to the fact that he's very hard of hearing. So trips like this one can seem to be either embarrassing or extremely humorous adventures, depending on my outlook. For example, an attractive young woman might return to the waiting room from the doctor's examining room and my father might think he's whispering when he says, as he did on this occasion, "Gee! Do you think those pants could be any more tight?"

For some reason, perhaps because I'd told myself it was coming, I found myself amused. I closed my eyes and smiled. *It's all material for stories.* I told myself. *It's all the lumber that W.O. Mitchell taught you about.* I opened my eyes and looked at the woman sitting across from us, who was clearly embarrassed for the girl and, also, I hoped, for me.

"That's my father!" I said, sounding as proud as a child introducing him to his teacher.

I sat back, thinking that the show was over for this trip, when a man not much older than I am walked into the clinic. Well dressed, slightly balding. He approached the receptionist and announced, for all of us to hear, "I HAVE A SKIN CONDITION AND I DON'T KNOW WHAT IT IS!"

I smiled at my dad. Even he had heard this, and I *knew* where the man would sit.

Yup, right next to me.

"HI! I HAVE A SKIN CONDITION!"

"Yes. I heard," I whispered—and he heard me, so I knew he wasn't hard of hearing.

Looking straight ahead, not at me, and in a much quieter voice, he asked, "Have they been here yet?"

"I'm sorry. Who?"

"The character assassins. Sometimes they get here before me. But if I'm quiet and don't tell anyone my plans, sometimes they don't come at all."

"I'm sorry, I don't understand."

"My wife—correction, my ex-wife—has hired a small group of people who look just like me. When she finds out my plans, say I've got a date, or I'm going shopping or something, she sends them out ahead of me and they'll act really strange, or just bad, and ruin any chance I've got with the girl or the store manager will tell me to leave before I even get to the frozen food section!"

"Oh, I see. Nope. No one looking like you has been here since we got here."

"That's good. So I'm moving out of my apartment and into a rest home soon. It'll be a lot cheaper for my kids, because, you know, I'm not working any more."

"It's good that it will be less expensive for your kids."

"Yes. And it'll be easier for me to get dates. There are a lot more women in rest homes than men, you know. I'll have my pick because I'm still pretty young."

"That's true."

"Getting dates is hard right now on account of me losing my licence and having to take the bus everywhere. Girls don't like to go on dates on the bus. I mean, I'd pay and everything, but they just don't want to take the bus. But at the rest home, I'd be living with them already! No bus!"

Without pausing, he said to the reception-ist, "HEY! I CAN'T WAIT AROUND HERE ANY MORE TODAY, OKAY? I'LL HAVE TO COME BACK MAYBE TOMORROW."

And with that, Walter—for that was his name—got up and left.

My father, who can sometimes surprise me with his sensitivity, looked at me, patted me on the knee and said, very quietly, "That man came in here needing just to talk with someone, and he chose you. An honour."

I wrote this story, which is true, because I haven't been quite sure how to tell some of the stories of students and community members who were dealing with mental health issues during my time with them. I don't want them to sound in any way pathetic, and I certainly don't want to make fun of them, although sometimes the things they say certainly do sound funny at the time. "I HAVE A SKIN CONDITION AND I DON'T KNOW WHAT IT IS!" being an example. And you knew where he was going to sit, the same way I did, didn't you?

***

Back when I taught Society: Challenge and Change, a course designed to introduce the disciplines of psychol-ogy, sociology and anthropology to grade eleven students, I invited a young man dealing with schizophrenia and his mother to talk to the class. I don't remember how I knew the two of them. I sat in the horseshoe arrangement of desks with my students; the young man sat next to me and his mother sat in the middle. She spoke quietly and earnestly about her son's condition. Both mother and son spoke about their struggles. Schizophrenia often emerges in a person's teenage years, so this was always a topic that fascinated the kids; having learned how common a condition it is, they always looked at each other and themselves, wondering if perhaps one of them was beginning to walk down that road.

My students were quiet and respectful. They asked real and thoughtful questions of both the mother and her son. It was one of many moments when I was both proud and happy to be a teacher.

Suddenly, the young man said, "It's happening right now! We have to leave! Yes! Now!"

The mother patted her son on the back of his hand. "I'm sorry, people. This has been lovely. Thank you very much for your understanding. God bless you."

"Just a minute ago! They were all there! All of them!"

And then they were gone—too quickly to thank, although one of my students had been prepared to thank them and give them each a school mug and pen set. "I'm sorry, Mr. Garlick. There just wasn't time to thank them!"

"That's all right, Sarah. I'll be sure to get them their gifts and give them our thanks. And they know how much we appreciated them. I'm very proud of you all right now."

Silence. From the whole class. For, well, really only a minute, but that's a really long time for a class to stay quiet. Then,

"He looked just like us... He could have been... might be... one of us. He just looked, well, normal..."

"That's the thing though, isn't it, Sir?" another student added. "They look normal because they *are* normal. They're just dealing with something they can't understand. Right?"

I had never been more proud of a group of students in my career, or proud to have had something to do with creating that moment.

After school that day, a student stuck his head in my doorway. "Sir? Do you have a minute?"

"Sure! Come on in."

"I just came by to…" his voice caught, "to… thank you." And then the tears started. Weeping. The kind of crying where you can't catch your breath and you can't talk: all you can do is cry. He gave me the biggest hug and wept into my shoulder. After about five minutes, he began to pull himself together. I gave him a few tissues and he apologized.

"No. No. It's fine. Sometimes you just have to cry."

He nodded, still not sure he could talk. Then, haltingly, "I'm the youngest child in my family by far. The next youngest is seven years older than me. I don't see my oldest brother… haven't seen him in years. Occasionally, he'll call, but only to speak to my mother, and only for a couple minutes. Just to check in and say he's all right. When he was about sixteen, he started to act… odd… and none of us, certainly not me—because I was, what, four? —understood what was happening to him. And then, one night, I don't know what time it was, I woke up and he was standing over me with a pillow in his hands. I wasn't scared or anything, I mean, he was my brother, right? He kept saying, 'Won't hurt. Won't hurt,' and then, just as he put the pillow on my face, my mother was there and she took the pillow away and walked him out of my room. He left that night, or the next morning, and I haven't seen him since. My mother was just so calm. And for years I've thought how much he must have hated me. And we've never ever talked about it. I think my mom thinks I don't remember. I've been carrying that around for all my life until today. But because of you, and today, I see now that maybe he doesn't hate me at all. He's just worried that maybe he'll hurt me. And my mother was so calm because he was still her son and still my brother." More tears. "So thank you."

***

Since that day, I've encountered a few students and people in the community who were clearly wrestling with mental demons. One student had to be withdrawn from school for his own safety and his parents' peace of mind. The last time I saw him, his father brought him into the school to say good-bye and to collect his things. They came into my office and sat down across from me. And then the boy was up, and standing next to me, patting me on the head. I shook his hand, which stopped him from petting me.

"I want to thank you for being so understanding about my boy. This isn't him right now."

The boy was giggling and drumming on my desk, stopping to lick his fingers and touch his tongue. A semester before he'd been on the honour roll. Great kid.

"Last night we woke up and he wasn't in bed. It was raining last night, remember? I found him two blocks away, in his pyjamas, walking backwards down the middle of the street. I'll bring him back to school as soon as we can, alright?"

The father stood up to shake my hand, and the student kissed me, hard, on the mouth.

I think of him often, and wonder how he's doing. Even in the '90s, there were effective treatments for schizophrenia, but sometimes the side effects could be as debilitating as the schizophrenia.

And now that I've retired, I think of other students. Students who, at the time, I thought of as belligerent, or annoying, or just plain "work" for me and my vice-principals, and I wonder if maybe I wasn't seeing them, but I was seeing the beginnings of their wrestling with their demons.

And if they were—I'm sorry for not understanding.

What's in a Name?

I apologize in advance if the reader has delicate sensibilities. There is, in this story, language that some might find offensive. I'm not writing this in order to offend. I'm just relating an experience. As Miss Wakely said, "An Anecdote. An event. This happened."

When you grow up with the surname "Garlick," you become—or, at least, *I* became—interested in, and respectful of, other people's names.

My peers, when we were kids, weren't respectful, as you would probably guess.

Throughout grade school and into high school, bullies thought they were being hilarious and original when they held their noses walking by my desk, or called me Garlic Bread. And because they were bullies, other kids had to at least pretend to also find it hilarious.

It helped a little when my father explained that Garlick was a profession name. It was older than the Norman Conquest, and the first Garlick on record was Luke the Garlic Monger, who came to England from France and became Luke Garlick. And that if I was to ever visit

London, England, I'd have to visit Garlick Heath. We shared our name with a street in London!

Strangely, it helped a bit more when my father explained that when he was a kid, his nickname was Stinky. Thankfully, to that point, this had not become my nick name as well. My bullies weren't that clever.

And so, as a teacher, I became very good at pronouncing names correctly when I saw them written out first. Depending on where my students came from, that was a skill that both impressed and endeared me to the affected students. I was, for example, the first teacher in Canada to correctly pronounce Brandigampola: short "i," emphasis on the second last syllable, Bran - di - gam - PO - la.

"Sir! You're the first teacher in Canada to correctly pronounce my name! Wow! That's going to be a topic of conversation at the dinner table tonight!"

Nshimyamana; Bhandiophadyay; Karelfloger; all pronounced correctly the first time.

And if I was stymied by one, say, one that began with "Xzy," had multiple consecutive consonants, and a silent vowel or two, I wouldn't even try. I'd just say, "Your name is fascinating to me! Please pronounce it for me until I can pronounce it correctly."

Names are important and people appreciate the effort.

Very occasionally in thirty-plus years, a student came to my class embarrassed by what they thought was going to happen, by what had probably happened before.

"Pronounce it however you want, Sir. It doesn't matter."

"Of course it matters! It's your name!" I'd say.

"No, really, I don't care. It doesn't matter."

But then I'd play my trump card. My winner. "Look. I grew up with the name Garlick. Do you have any idea how cruel kids can be when they find out your name is Garlick? I want to pronounce your name correctly, okay?"

"Oh… Zin-SHEEN-ee-yay."

"Zin-SHEEN-ee-yay… Cool!"

Several teachers came to me for short tutorials on the correct pronunciation of the names on their attendance lists. This made me proud for two reasons: one, I was being recognized as an expert in something by other teachers; and two, it meant that I was part of a staff that cared about their kids that much. No one called all their boys "Dick" and all their girls "Jane," for example, which a retired principal I know thought was cute. And no one called everyone younger than he was "Sparky," which a retired teacher I know also thought was cute.

A student's name was a student's name. And it deserved to be pronounced as correctly as Garlick or Smith or Jones. And really, after a bit of practice, almost *all* names roll pretty well and easily off the tongue.

With just one exception in thirty-five years.

One. In thirty-five years.

Before he came to Canada, I'm guessing there was no issue. I have no idea how it was handled after he left our school. I hope it was handled with the grace and common sense my students showed.

It was his name after all.

It was a short, two syllable, Cambodian name. As short as possible to say.

And as a teenager, I had no problem saying it in certain situations. I still don't, I'll admit.

His name was Phuc Me. And yes, it's pronounced exactly as you're reading it.

"Well, Phuc Me!" I said to myself, reading over my class list. How to deal with this?

At least it was an English as a Second Language class. Not everyone would hear the name as something a teacher shouldn't be saying. Still, the boy would know by now that his *name* was something that, if shouted in anger, could get a kid suspended; could, in some circumstances, start a fight.

But whether it was because the class was an ESL class, or the kids were just that much more mature than I'd been in high school, or that he was just such a nice kid, no one had any problem saying his first name like any other first name. Their thirty-something year old teacher found it *very* funny on a continuing basis.

"Come on! Phuc! You know this!" (Mr. Garlick bites his cheek to keep from laughing.)

"Phuc! We want Phuc in our group!"

If he wasn't paying attention, someone would always say, helpfully, "PHUC! PHUC ME!

And I never got used to hearing fifteen-year-old girls saying that if he was having difficulty they'd be happy to help Phuc out.

But for me, it was only a semester with him.

And because of his age and previous experience, he graduated only a couple years later.

Graduation that year was held at one of Windsor's largest auditoriums. More than 200 graduates and more than 800 guests attended, including our director, the mayor, and two trustees.

Each student walked across the stage and had their name read out by Mr. Richard Saunders, one of the nicest men I've ever known and the closest person to Mr. Rogers who I've ever met. He had never, to my knowledge, taught this student.

And no one prepped him.

Like me, he was particularly good at pronouncing student names and never asked for help. Maybe, I thought, maybe he doesn't even pre-read the list.

And so… We pick things up at the letter "L."

"Charlene Longpre." *Clap, clap, clap, clap.*

"Timothy Luxford." *Clap,clap, clap, clap.*

"Arthur Mason." *Clap, clap, clap, clap.*

Skip on down, Garlick. We know what's coming.

Richard Saunders is stuck for only a second. And then,…

"*Mister* Me." *Clap, clap, clap, Garlick giggles, clap, clap, clap.*

Year Two, Day One

My first-period class in my second year of teaching was a senior History class. I'm pretty sure that somewhere else in this book you can read why, in Year One, I only taught the junior grades. While there are joys to teaching grade ten History, it's completely different than teaching kids in their senior year.

For one thing, in grade ten, many kids are there because they have to be. Grade ten History is a required course, one that many kids *know* they're going to hate. It can take a significant amount of time to convince kids that they might actually enjoy your class. For another thing, kids in grade ten have been in high school for a full year: think they know "the ropes," and act that way.

Kids in grade twelve, though, they *do* know the ropes, and if they're taking History, it's almost always because they want to.

And I should also add that teaching period one is different than teaching period two, or three or four. People act differently at 8:50 in the morning than they do just before lunch or just before the school bell rings to release them at the end of the day.

They also come to your class in smaller groups, or even singly, depending on when they get to school in the morning—if you happen to be one of those teachers that spends the early morning in your classroom with your door open. I forget what I was working on that morning. Lesson plans were done. I may have been writing out my attendance register. That particular memory is gone—

"Good morning, Sir. My name is Vladimir, and no offense, but I won't be staying in your class, okay? The computer gave your class to me, but I don't really want to take it. I came early to see if I could drop it, but Guidance says I need to be here this morning, and they'll fix things for me later today. Okay? I'll just sit here at the back."

"Sure, Vladimir. What are you going to take instead?"

"Nothing at all! I can take a spare! It'll let me sleep in for a whole semester!"

"Oh! That's kind of hard for me to compete with, isn't it?"

"Yeah. So, no offense…"

"None taken."

I went back to working on what I'd been working on.

"So what are you going to be teaching in this class?"

"Modern history. We'll start with the French Revolution and work our way forward, getting as close to now as possible. The great thing about *this* class is that we don't have to finish the curriculum. If the class finds something particularly interesting, we can continue to work on it. We don't have to finish anything off."

"Cool… Doesn't beat sleeping in though…"

"I guess not."

Then Sophia Angelina walked in. To me, a happily married, thirty-five-year-old man, Sophia was one of the most beautiful young women I'd ever seen. I cannot imagine what Vladimir thought when she walked in.

"Good morning, Mr. Garlick! I'm Sophia Angelina. I've been looking forward to this class for months! You taught my sister last year, and she really enjoyed your class. She told me to say Hi for her. Vlad! You're here too? This is going to be great!"

And then, before Sophia could even choose a seat, Emilia Santos walked in. New to the school, new to the country, Emilia was every bit as pretty as Sophia.

"Mr. Garlick? Am I in the right room? Is this Modern History?"

"Yes, it is. Sit anywhere you'd like."

She shook my hand and introduced herself. And then she shook Sophia's hand and Vladimir's hand and took a seat.

The class filled up pretty quickly after that. Thirty-two kids.

Vladimir got an A in the class. Never missed a day.

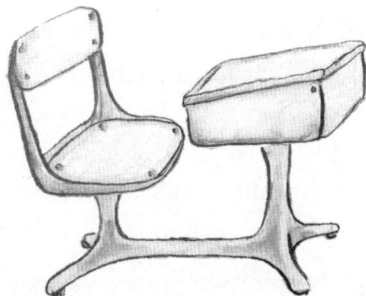

Oliver Crombie

Oliver Crombie died this week. I read his obituary in the newspaper. Apparently, he was a stand up guy, loved by his family, the people in his neighbourhood and his golfing buddies. I wouldn't have recognized him from the picture that had been chosen, I'm guessing, by his children: a young man in a baseball cap, squinting a bit against the sun or the flash of the camera. It looked as though the cap was part of a uniform, and not a fashion statement.

When I knew him, he was much older.

The obituary didn't mention that he'd once been a teacher and spent more than thirty years at the same school. But I guess that's appropriate. He'd retired in

1995, over twenty-five years ago, and by that time he wasn't really much of a teacher anymore, just a bitter man verging on old age, no longer even reticent about displaying his bigotry and prejudice towards the very people who were in his charge. The more I thought about it, the more I thought he'd written much of his own obituary and chosen the photo himself.

I met him in the staff room during my second week in the school. I was the new kid, the young department head who still had his head in the clouds.

"You know," he said to the room, "I didn't mind the Boat People when they arrived. I mean, they looked different, but it turned out they were hard workers. Clean. Tried hard in class, too. Wanted to fit in. But these new ones, the ones from the Middle East? You can keep the whole lot of them. A dead loss, in my opinion. They don't contribute to the school at all. Not on any teams. Not on any clubs. Any of 'em."

"Have you asked them?" I asked him.

"What?"

"Have you asked any of those students? Maybe they're scared. Maybe they don't think they'll be accepted. Maybe they think they're not wanted and they won't fit in."

"What have they got to be scared of? They're in Canada, for God's sake! They're here, aren't they?"

"I suppose... But I wonder what they went through to get here, what they're going through right now."

"Aw, geez! Is everyone listening to this? Hey everyone! Meet the new bleeding-heart teacher!" He snorted, dismissing both my comment and me.

"I wonder, Mr. Crombie. What clubs and teams are you in charge of?" I asked.

"What?"

"What clubs and teams do you sponsor?"

"Don't be a smart-ass!"

"I'm not. I'm the new kid, remember? I just don't know... But I think I can guess."

"Smart-ass."

And with that, he got up from the table and left the room.

I didn't say anything and resumed eating my sandwich, not making eye contact with anyone else.

"Hey... Dave? Thanks for that." This from Derek Parker, a teacher not much younger that Mr. Crombie.

"For?"

"Oliver's not a bad guy. He used to be a fine teacher. We don't know what happened to him, but we've all noticed the change. It must have happened slow and gradual. Lately, he's just gone sour. Time for him to start thinking about retirement."

"Hmmph! It was *time* a couple-few years ago!" said Penny North.

"Well, in any case, I'm guessing we won't have to listen to any more of that garbage for a while, at least while you're here. Thanks, Dave." Derek Parker finished the conversation.

I don't remember ever speaking to Mr. Crombie again, though I probably did. "Good Morning." "Good Evening." "Hi." That kind of thing. But we avoided each other. On my side, it was because I didn't want to be around that kind of negativity and prejudice.

On his side, it was because I'd caught him out, pricked his little balloon of bigotry and made it uncomfortable for him to spout off in the staff room.

He retired at the end of that school year with no fanfare. He told the principal he didn't want a party or for anyone to make a fuss. I think he was afraid that we wouldn't make a fuss, and wouldn't throw him a party.

But maybe we would have. Thirty years is a long time and deserves some recognition. And he was an older staff member. What's that expression? "You've got to go to someone's funeral, or maybe they won't come to yours."

Anyway, I wouldn't have gone.

But now, all these years later, and years since I've retired, I realize that Oliver Crombie was a mentor to me as a teacher, if only as a model of something I didn't ever want to do or become.

And so, Mr. Crombie, where ever you are, whether you're playing that new course with the golfing buddies who passed on before you in heaven, or somewhere else— thank you. RIP.

Part Three:
David as Vice-Principal and Principal

Why I Bought a Cell Phone in the First Place

I remember a few years ago—well, actually, more than a few now—visiting Europe with my wife and laughing at all the people we saw using their cell phones in public. Cell phones had yet to become omnipresent in North American society.

"Hey, look at me! I'm *really* important!" we'd say, chuckling.

"Can you imagine," we'd go on to say to each other, over our continental breakfasts, "*wanting* to and actually being connected all the time? What could be so important, unless you're a world leader or a surgeon or something?"

Well, now we know. Cheese for $4.88 is that important. A third reminder about your music lesson is that important. And yes, people do want and need to be connected that much. Twenty-four hours a day, seven days a week. Parents call their children at school to ask them how their day is going, and to tell them what's for supper, and yes, to remind them about their music lesson after school. I lost count of the number of parents who told me they *needed* to have that instant connection with their children. My mother just wanted me home before the street lights came on—and, when I was a bit older, just to try not to wake her up when I got home. And she loved me just as much as today's parents love their kids. Still does, as a matter of fact.

I get it, though. Times have changed. And cell phones aren't just phones: they're mini-computers that connect you to the internet and all the information in the world. And they fit right in your pocket or purse. So while I resisted the allure of the cell phone longer than most, I admit to being a convert now.

What was the tipping point, you ask? Why did I decide to move into the second half of the twentieth century? I was a vice-principal in a core area high school. A lot of my families didn't even have telephones, let alone cell phones, or at least, they didn't answer them when I called. So at the end of each school day, I'd prepare a list of parents I needed to speak with, but hadn't been able to reach throughout the day. Maybe I had to inform them about an upcoming school council meeting, or congratulate them on raising a fine daughter or son when a student had done something remarkable at school, or, as often as not, I had to inform them that their child was suspended and was not to come to school the next day. I'd hand the parent the written suspension letter, explain what it said and what had happened, and save the school the postage. At the end of each day, I'd take my list and head out the back door.

Almost immediately, I'd be accosted by a group of elementary students on bicycles, skateboards, and roller blades. "Who you gonna expend this time, Mr. Garlick? I'll bet it's my brother, he's a jerk! What'd he do *this* time?"

I was always pleasant with these kids, ignoring their questions and asking them about their days. As soon as I turned up a street that wasn't theirs, they'd continue on their way. "See you, Mr. Garlick! Have a good day!"

Once, I walked up to a house with the screen door closed, but the inner door wide open, and the TV blaring away. Judge Judy was passing sentence. I rang the door bell and wasn't surprised when no one responded, the TV was *that* loud. I knocked on the door. Waited. No response. I rapped again and called out, pretty loudly, "Hello!" And from way down the hallway came this cute little boy in a diaper or those pull-up things. He was pretty sure on his feet, but was certainly no more than two years old.

"Hi little man!" Big smiles from both of us. "Is your mom home?" Judge Judy had given way to a commercial about hand cream which was even louder.

"No!"

"Is your Dad home, then?"

"No!"

"Is… anybody home with you?" My smile faded.

The toddler giggled and ran back down the hallway. I stood there, waiting for someone to come back with the little boy, but nobody came.

What was I to do? If I left, I was maybe leaving a two-year-old unattended and everything that might mean. If I went into the house, I was trespassing, maybe even breaking and entering. I checked the door—yes, unlocked—and if I entered, I just knew that at that moment someone would come out and scream, or chase me up the street, or worse. And if I left now, knowing the screen door was unlocked, I also knew the toddler would come back to the door looking for the nice man in the suit and he'd get hit by a train or smoke cigarettes or join a gang. I just didn't know what to do.

If only there was some way I could, maybe call the police? My principal? Even my wife, so I could cry a little. Suddenly, those cell phones didn't seem so silly.

I rapped on the door again, and called out. The boy's little head peaked out from... I don't know... the kitchen? Where he was playing with knives? Or maybe the stove top was on, covered in pots of hot grease? I have a fertile but pretty realistic imagination.

He toddled back up the hall to me. Used cars were apparently really cheap and available for no money down. "Listen, could you do me a favour and turn the TV down?"

I expected him to pick up a remote control, I guess. I did *not* expect him pull out the bottom drawer of the chest that the TV was sitting on, and *climb* towards the huge screen that I realized, at that moment, could (would?) fall over and crush him to death.

"Uhh hey! It's okay! Don't bother!"

"Just a middit!" he shouted back to me.

And then the volume was turned down and he was running back to get his next instructions from me.

"Whew! Okay! Good job! Now I need you to cover your ears because I'm going to shout *really* loudly, okay?"

And he did. And I did. For about, really, thirty seconds. Thirty very long seconds.

And then my student, the sixteen-year-old girl I was there to remind about her one-day suspension, or inform her parents about, came up from the basement.

"Oh hi, Mr. Garlick! I was just downstairs doing my homework." No, she wasn't.

After admonishing her for leaving her little brother unattended for so long and hand-delivering the letter of suspension I'm pretty sure her parents never saw, I marched straight back to the school, got in my car, drove home and told my wife, "We're going to the mall after supper. I need a cell phone!"

I was that important now.

Zamir

When I was at W.D. Lowe Secondary School and later at J.L. Forster, I hated calling parents at home. Not because I didn't want to talk with them, but because, although their children moved through the different levels of the English as a Second Language Program, the parents rarely did.

Sometimes the parents went to school at night and learned English at pretty much the same rate as their children. Sometimes they already knew more English than their children and kept ahead of them. Sometimes, though—often—usually—the parents I spoke with were the ones who stayed at home throughout the day. I have no idea what their lives were like from day to day, but I did know that they weren't learning English.

"DON'T SPEAK ENGLISH," they would shout into the phone, upon picking it up and hearing someone other than a relative from back home.

"Hi, Mrs. Nishani! This is Dave Garlick, from Fors—"

"DON'T SPEAK ENGLISH!"

I hated that. Where could I go from there? I didn't speak their language. They didn't speak mine. It wasn't as though I had an interpreter sitting next to me.

In Zamir's case, there was only one other adult in the whole city who spoke both his language and English. One translator. Well, one that I knew of, and he worked throughout the day.

That man had, almost literally, saved Zamir's life a few months earlier, along with his brother Vjosa, and four other young men who had arrived at school with no English, and having not attended any school for more than four years.

Three beautiful young Arab girls had come into my office one day and asked if they could close the door. "Sir? Please understand. We don't want anyone to get into any trouble. We just want them to stop. We don't think they even mean any harm, really, but we've asked them to stop and well, if our brothers find out what they're doing, they'll kill them."

The new students, who were being implored to stop, had seemingly learned everything they knew about North American culture from watching old Marlon Brando movies. They leaned up against telephone poles and, as young women passed, they'd kiss the air and say one of their very few English sentences: "Hey Baby! You—me?" and then kiss the air again.

This amount of disrespect could, depending on the girls and the brothers involved, earn Zamir and his young friends a severe beating.

I forget how we found the translator, or even what his name was. He was a very nice man who wanted to help us and the new members of the community who were putting themselves at risk. We arranged for a "Town Hall

Meeting" of the entire community of newcomers to meet in our auditorium. They all came. For some reason, the young men sat apart from their parents, in the front row. The parents couldn't see the boys' reactions to what I was saying, or the words of the translator, but I could see both the young men's faces and their parents'.

"Thank you very much for coming this evening. My name is David Garlick. I'm the assistant principal of the school." Confusion followed by understanding as the translator repeated. Head nods. Smiles. "We're very happy you could join us, and we're also happy that your children are coming to our school." People looked to the translator as he said what I just said, and then looked back to me, again smiling.

I'll interrupt my story to tell you that this group of people were refugees from the Albanian part of what was Serbia and was now known as Kosovo. Their lives had been hellish for a number of years, their journey both to Canada and to this point in their lives, fraught with danger. Many had seen relatives killed and watched their homes destroyed. One student had found his own high school principal's murdered body by the side of a stream. They'd been promised safety and a fresh start in Canada, and, so far at least, they'd experienced that.

These were grateful and hard-working adults. And these were students with huge learning gaps, some of whom hadn't been to school in years. They were happy to be some place safe. And our teachers were not as hard-nosed or strict as theirs had been previously. While the students enjoyed this, this kindness had been mistaken for weakness and a lack of standards.

"But we have some concerns, and we need your help." Again, they looked to the translator, and their smiles turned to looks of concern. What was the problem and how could they help?

"Your sons are good people. We really like working with them. But there are issues, particularly after school." Again, concern from the parents. The boys in the front row, were a different matter, punching each other in the shoulders, trying hard, mostly successfully, not to laugh out loud.

"After school, before they go home, they stand out front of the school and bother some of the girls." Mothers and fathers showed me a variety of reactions as this was translated for them. Concern, disbelief, worry. Some had an "I was afraid this would happen" type of look on their faces—an acceptance of what I was saying, and a "How am I going to deal with this at home?" look. It's amazing how much you can read from a facial expression.

The boys found this absolutely hilarious! They could no longer contain their sense of mirth at the situation and what I was saying. Two laughed out loud.

"While I'm sure the boys mean no harm," my voice louder, above their laughter, "they have no idea of the danger they're putting themselves in." The laughter subsided to giggles as my voice got louder, and then stopped completely when what I said was translated. They knew all about danger. They thought they'd left it behind, but here was this friendly vice-principal using that word—and he was using it about them. Now the entire audience looked concerned.

"I'm not talking about suspensions or school punishment. The girls they are bothering, by cat-calling, whistling and winking, are members of large families concerned about honour and how their sisters and daughters are treated." I had no idea if "cat-calling" would be easy to translate, but I found out that the word "honour" was very important to all of them. They were all *very* concerned now.

"If this behaviour continues—" and here I looked directly at the boys— "If this behaviour continues, you will be beaten by the brothers and fathers. You may even be killed. And I cannot stop that."

Nobody defended their sons. Nobody questioned the honesty of the girls. Nobody asked about the police, or punishment for the brothers and fathers. Nobody asked if I was overstating the case or counter-threatened. Whether it was their own personal experience, or whether I and the translator had presented the case that well, no one questioned me. The translator looked at me and asked, "To be clear, if the behaviour stops, the boys—they will live?" I nodded. The parents began telling the translator they would speak to their sons that night. It would never happen again. They were all very sorry. They asked if they could apologize to the girls. They told me that this was not how their sons were raised. They were all very sorry. It would never happen again. They left the auditorium together, arms around their sons.

And it never did happen again. I had many other issues with the Kosovo Kids, but never once did they have anything to do with treating a girl with disrespect.

Anyway, I started this by saying that I hated calling the parents of refugees. And the title of this piece is "Zamir." I often had to call Zamir's mother to try to tell her that I was sending Zamir home. Sometimes he'd learned a new and inappropriate word, clearly knew that it was inappropriate, and then he'd use it in a sentence—repeatedly—in a very loud voice during class. Usually, the rest of the class had learned the word a few weeks or days before, and knew they shouldn't use it at school. Usually, they were shocked and offended, or claimed to be. Zamir would be sent home for the rest of the day. "I sorry. It not will happen."

Sometimes he'd get himself involved in… *altercations*. They weren't really fights. Pushing matches. Poor but effective attempts at swearing: "Bastard! Pull my fingers!"

"What did you say to me?" said the young man who Zamir had bumped into in a crowded hallway.

"Your mother!"

Then there would be pushing and shoving and both would end up in my office and go home for the rest of the day. I won't claim that this was the most effective, or even appropriate consequence, but it's what I did. I'd call the young English-speaker's home, inform his parents of what had happened, and then he'd go home.

And then I had to call Zamir's mother.

Her English, as I implied above, was very weak. I could only say, "Zamir, fight, home." I couldn't trust Zamir to explain to his mother what had happened. I wouldn't know what he was telling her in any case. My three word sentence would have to do.

But once, once, she wasn't home when I called, and I had the opportunity to leave a message!

"Mrs. Nishani? This is David Garlick, from Forster. I'm sorry to have to call you to tell you that I have to send Zamir home this afternoon. He was involved in an altercation at lunch. No one was hurt, but this cannot be tolerated."

And then Zamir went home. And when he got home, his mother played the message for him.

(The conversation which follows was originally in Albanian.)

"Zamir? I think this is Mr. Garlick leaving a message. What is he saying?"

Zamir listened to the message.

"You're right! That *is* Mr. Garlick! He's calling to tell you what a good job I did on the Geography test today!"

She kissed him on the forehead and congratulated him. He went off to his room for a nap.

And then, twenty minutes later, Zamir's younger sister, Bujare, came racing into the house. "Mom! Mom! Did Zamir tell you about the fight?"

Mrs. Nishani didn't say a word. She walked over to Zamir's door and locked him in. I can only surmise why Zamir's door was fitted so it could be locked from the outside.

How do I know these conversations occurred? The next morning, after Zamir had spent the night locked in his room and had probably not had supper, or had eaten it cold, Bujare knocked on my office door to speak with me.

"That boy! What am I going to do with him?" she said. "I give him *so* many chances!"

Two Names That Always Make My Wife Smile

I was an administrator for seventeen years and taught for sixteen years before that. My wife lived with me for twenty-seven of those years, and listened patiently to my stories at the end of each day, usually either being sympathetic, outraged, or amused, as I intended. Now, after thirty-two years, there are two student names I only have to mention to make her smile.

One is Mohamed. Mohamed of the Split Head. And the other is Amir. Little Amir.

Mohamed

Late one evening in June, I was just getting ready to leave at the end of a long day when the phone rang. It was 7:00 p.m. I asked myself, "Who would call the school at 7:00 p.m. at the end of a long day in June?" I knew there was only one way to find out the answer to that question, so I took the call.

"Hello, Mr. Garlick? This is Mohamed calling."

"I'm sorry, Mohamed, you're going to have to give me a bit more to go on than that."

Mohamed was a very common name at Forster. As I recall, we had more than thirty different Mohameds that year, with different spellings, and then an additional number of fathers with that name as well. Plus there were all the other Mohameds I'd worked with at Lowe. All tolled, there were maybe a hundred people who could have been on the other end of the phone line.

"Oh, sorry. This is Mohamed of the Split Head."

I smiled a big smile. "How can I help you, Mohamed?"

Back at the end of my second week as VP at Forster, I was still waiting for my first suspension. There had been no fights, no altercations, no truancy—nothing—and I was beginning to wonder if Forster really needed a vice-principal. But at the end of that second week, I was outside as lunch was ending when my secretary called me on my walkie-talkie. "Mr. Garlick, something's happened outside the library. They need you right away. At least two students are involved and there's a lot of blood."

Finally! A fight! I get to do my job! I ran up the stairs and down the hall towards the library. Two kids were sitting on opposite sides of the hallway, each being tended to by a teacher. One had blood pouring down his face.

"Sorry man! I just didn't see you coming!"

"Me either! I just didn't want to be late!"

It turned out that Mohamed and the other boy, Tom, were both trying, desperately, to get to class on time. They each rounded the corner going in opposite directions and smacked their heads together. I called my secretary and asked her to call Mohamed's and Tom's parents and have them meet me at the medical clinic downstairs (how lucky was I to have a medical clinic *in my school?*).

By this time, Tom was sporting an almost literal goose-egg-sized lump on his forehead, and Mohamed had blood pouring down his face, which a handful of paper towels wasn't doing much to staunch.

We only had to wait a couple-few minutes before being seen. The boys' parents arrived as Mohamed was being stitched up. The compression cut required, I think, five or six stitches, and Mohamed's father was very grateful for our quick action.

Tom was upset that he wasn't going to be allowed to go to football practice that evening, but his parents were also happy with how things turned out.

Neither boy, by the way, ever caused me a moment of work after that day. I think they became good friends. And although neither of them made the honour roll, they both graduated and went off to college. Mohamed gave himself the moniker, "Mohamed of the Split Head," and that's how I referred to him from then on. I was very happy one day, years later, to run into him (figuratively) at the mall when I was with my wife. "I'm pleased to meet you, Mrs. Garlick. My name is Mohamed of the Split Head."

And why was Mohamed of the Split Head calling me at 7:00 p.m. on an evening in June, ten years after he'd graduated? He was wondering if I would write him a letter of reference. "Why yes, I'd be happy and proud to do that for you, Mohamed."

Little Amir

I was called to an English as a Second Language classroom because, apparently, there'd been an assault in class. I was met at the door by the teacher who said, "I have no idea what happened to cause it. All of a sudden, three boys got smacked across the face—and hard!"

I walked in and the class fell silent.

This was a level B class, which meant that the students had all been in Canada for at least a semester, and had acquired one class worth of English instruction. I'd have to speak clearly and use words everyone would understand.

"Who was smacked across the face?" All twenty students raised their hands.

"No. I mean, which of you were hit?" Three hands went up.

"And who did the smacking? Who did the hitting?" Everyone pointed at one little boy, the smallest student in the class—Little Amir.

Amir joined me in the hallway. "Amir, what happened? Why did you smack those boys?"

"These kids? Theytouchmyass."

"Pardon? Do you mean they hit you?" I swung my hand, pretending to hit something.

"No! Theytouchmyass!"

"Pinch?" Holding my hand up, pinching my thumb and forefinger together.

"No! Theytouchmyass!" At this point, he touched *my* ass with his hand. "Like that!"

"Oh! Did you tell them not to do that? That you didn't like it?"

"Yes! I told them don't touchmyass. If you touchmyass, I'll tell Mr. Garlick!"

"So what happened?"

"They touchedmyass and I *smackedtheirfaces*!"

"Amir… You can't smack people across the face…"

"I didn't!"

"You just told me you did!"

"I smacked *one* boy's face!"

"Amir…"

"Okay…"

"Go to my office, and I'll meet you there in a few minutes. All right?"

I called the three boys out into the hall.

"Okay boys, why are you touching Amir's bum?"

They all smiled, clearly embarrassed and amused at the same time. Their VP had said "bum." And their VP clearly knew what had happened. They looked at each other and then at me. "It's fun."

"Well, it's not going to happen any more, is it?" This was not really a question. I was not giving them an option.

"No, Sir. Amir's not in trouble, is he? He warned us. And we should have stopped. And it didn't hurt that much. We won't do it again. And he won't hit us again."

And they didn't. And he didn't.

Four Short Short Stories

Or, as Miss Wakely would say, "These are anecdotes. Events. They actually happened."

Story One

Shortly before my first day as an acting vice-principal, Elver Peruzzo, my principal and friend, took me out for a beer. "I want to thank you again for taking this job on, Dave. I don't want to think about what this coming year would be like if I had to teach a brand new vice-principal all about Lowe Secondary School and its kids."

"Well, you're going to have to teach me what it means to be a vice-principal. I've never actually talked with one about what they do from day to day, and I've never been one to worry too much about student discipline. Never had to. In the six years I've been here, I've only sent one kid to the VP, and that was you, because you looked so tired…"

"I've never heard this story."

"You must have been dealing with some pretty serious stuff and you just looked beat. And this was before school had even started for the day. So I sent one of my best kids down to see you with a note that introduced him to you, saying that ninety percent of the kids were just like him, and asking you to keep that in mind."

"Now I remember! But Dave, as VP, you're going to be working with the ten percent, and it *is* tiring. The truth is that those kids—the ten percent—they need a teacher like you. But you won't be getting a lot of positive feedback from them. In fact, you won't *really* be doing your job until somebody tells you to f--- off."

By this time, I'd been teaching for sixteen years, and no one had *ever* told me to f--- off. While I didn't exactly disbelieve Elver, I thought that maybe things would be different for me. I knew almost all the kids in the school, except the kids in grade nine, and everyone knew that I was a caring teacher who wanted only the best for them. And the kids in grade nine were all new and they'd be too scared to swear at me, right?

I was right for the first three weeks or so. I was busy, but the kids all seemed to appreciate what I was trying to do, and that I was learning the job as I went.

But then I had to suspend Bryce McEnany. I forget why, or for how long. I forget how I said it, but I *do* remember his response. "F--- you, Mr. Garlick!" (He said the whole expression.) And then he walked out of the office.

I sat there for about two minutes after he left. Then I walked out into the main office. The attendance secretary, Lorie Schofield, said, "Well, Bryce was pretty angry, wasn't he?"

I just nodded.

And then I walked across the main office to Elver's door, which was closed. I knocked lightly and then opened the door. Elver was meeting with a superintendent and a parent, I don't know what about.

"Yes, Mr. Garlick? Can I help you?"

"No, Sir. I just wanted to let you know that I'm doing my job."

Elver smiled. I smiled back and closed the door.

Story Two

Once, when I was a vice-principal, as kids were heading off to class first thing in the morning, ahead of the bell:

"What's the matter, Amy? You don't look very happy today. I'm used to seeing you with a big smile on your face!"

"I'm sorry, Mr. Garlick. I didn't get any sleep at all last night. My little brother was arrested by the police. Right out of the house! I'm worried sick about him. He's just sixteen…"

"I'm sorry to hear that, Amy. Well, if he's just sixteen and what he did wasn't *that* serious, I'm sure he'll be home very soon."

"That's what my mother says, too. Still, I can't help but be worried. This might wake him up though. He quit school on his birthday and he's been hanging out with some kids we don't know…"

"Well, I'll bet that by the time you get home from school, he'll be there waiting for you."

"I hope you're right, Sir. I'll let you know tomorrow what happened. My little brother's a good kid. Just a bit of a knucklehead sometimes."

Later that afternoon, just as kids were settling into their classes after lunch, a young man I'd never seen before knocked on my office door.

"Are you Mr. Garlick, Sir? My sister talks about you a lot. Says you're a straight up guy and pretty nice too. Would it be possible for me to see her for a minute? It's really important."

"Are you Amy's brother?"

"Yes Sir. I've been a bit of a jerk and I'd like to talk to her for just a minute. Please?"

"Give me a minute. I'll go get her for you. All right?"

I went to get Amy from her science class and we speed-walked back to my office. "Thanks for coming to get me, Mr. Garlick. I've been worried sick about him!"

Amy's brother was waiting in the hall for her. She ran and threw her arms around him. "You big jerk! I've been worried sick!"

"Yeah, thanks. You got an extra smoke or two?"

"A smoke! Mr. Garlick said you said it was important!" Amy looked at me, clearly both confused and upset with her brother.

"Hey! I haven't had a smoke since yesterday afternoon! This *is* important!"

Story Three

After the tragedy of 9/11, my high school took part in an initiative called Boots Across the Border. I forget whether it was local, provincial, or national. Anyway, as my father was a firefighter, I borrowed one of his work boots and went from class to class collecting donations for the surviving firefighters who'd been injured when the towers collapsed, and for the families of the firefighters who had perished.

I did this for two or three days; I forget how much money we raised, but it was more than any other school. I was asked to attend a special religious service to honour the firefighters who had died, and present the firemen's pastor from Detroit with our cheque.

Because my school was the Board's English as a Second Language School, we had a significant number of Muslim students. I thought it important to draw everyone's attention to this at a time when Muslims were beginning to experience the full force of Islamophobia in the United States, and, to a lesser extent, in Canada. Our Muslim students were as horrified as anyone else about the attack on New York, and were just as eager to help raise money for the firefighters.

I asked Mohamed Naseri to accompany me and help me present the cheque. Mohamed was an honour student, a member of Canada's military, and one of the most honourable young men I've ever had the privilege to know. He was also a devout Muslim. He agreed immediately.

While we were driving to the church, it became clear that Mohamed was nervous.

"This is going to be all right, isn't it? They won't mind having a Muslim in attendance?"

"It will be fine, Mohamed. You'll see. They'll be as proud of you as I am."

"And they won't mind me being in uniform?" He was wearing his dress military outfit and looked incredibly sharp.

"No. They won't mind."

"I've never been in a Catholic church before. You're sure they won't mind a Muslim being there?"

"They won't mind."

When we got to the church, I introduced myself to the parish priest, and then introduced him to Mohamed. "I can't tell you how proud I am of your school for what they've done." the priest said. "And Mohamed? I'm so happy Mr. Garlick chose you to be here. I think it's important for everyone to see that it doesn't make a difference if you're Protestant, Catholic, Islamic, Jewish or Buddhist. Everyone is the same in the eyes of God."

Mohamed became much more calm after this. When we were seated, he began to ask me dozens of questions about the church itself and the service we were about to be part of. As we looked at the order of the service, we saw where we fit into it and the list of dignitaries who would be present: the mayor and councillors, firefighters from around North America, and my own father would be there from the Windsor Fire Department. I forget who all else, but I do remember that the firemen's pastor from Detroit was to be there to accept the cheque and deliver a special homily. As I looked around the church, I tried to point out anyone I recognized to Mohamed.

In spite of the number of people in the church, there was only one person of colour dressed as a priest, so I said, very quietly to Mohamed, "I can't be certain, but I think that's the pastor from Detroit."

"Oh…"

Then, after about twenty seconds, he said, "I'm sorry, Mr. Garlick, but I have to say that I don't think you should be talking that way in church. That's not something to say in church."

I was confused for a second or two, thinking back over all the things we'd been talking about over the last few minutes. Then it became clear and I smiled at him.

"I said, 'I can't be certain, but I think that's the *pastor* from Detroit.'"

"Oh! Oh, well, that's all right then."

Story Four

The first thing I did when I found out that Angela Safranyos would be my new vice-principal was invite her and her family over for dinner. I'd known her for three years at the time, having been VP myself at Forster when she was head of business there. And she replaced me as VP at Forster, when I became principal at Western.

We never had any issues that I was aware of during that time, but by the same token, I wasn't completely sure what she thought of me, and whether or not she was looking forward to working with me again.

Anyway, she, her husband, and their almost impossibly cute five-year-old daughter came over for dinner one evening that summer. We were having a very enjoyable time, and after dinner we retired to the living room. I excused myself to go to the kitchen to refresh everyone's drinks.

I was just pouring the mixers when I felt a tap on my elbow. The almost impossibly cute five-year-old had very quietly followed me into the kitchen. She'd been wonderful all evening: polite, respectful, and funny. She looked around the kitchen and then looked behind her, clearly ready to share a secret or two. Then she motioned me to bend over so she could whisper in my ear.

"Mr. Garlick, do you know what my mother calls you at home?"

I thought, "Do I want to hear this? Angela and I are going to have to work together for at least a year. What if she calls me Doofus Garlick? Or worse? Why is she calling me *anything* at home—in front of her daughter? I like Angela! And I respect her opinion." But I responded almost as quietly,

"No. No I don't. What does your mother call me at home?"

Once again, she looked to the left, then she looked to the right, then she checked behind her. Good. Still alone. She whispered,

"She calls you Dave!"

Animals

I became a teacher because I was good with kids and I was also good with History and English. I became a principal because it turned out I was also pretty good with adults. At no time was I asked if I was particularly good with animals. I had no idea the number and variety of animals I'd deal with over the years. I'm not suggesting for a moment that I ever viewed my students as animals. I'm talking about the four-legged kind, the types with wings, and some with no legs at all. When taken as a group, they made up quite the menagerie.

So, in no particular order:

Squirrels and Bats

One of the things I always found pleasant about being an administrator was being in a school building all by myself. There's a feeling of... I don't know... importance, when you're given the pass-codes to turn off the alarm system for a massive building. And an empty school is a very interesting place. Typically, I'd be by myself in my office on weekends. I'd enter by the back door, turn off the alarm system, walk straight to my office, and work there, in the peace and quiet, for five or six hours. Occasionally, I'd walk through the school, taking myself on a solo tour.

Once, on a Saturday morning, during my first month as vice-principal of Forster Secondary School, I took myself on such a tour. I left my office, walked past the library, turned left at the staff room, walked up the five steps to the T wing, and turned the corner just in time to see a squirrel running down the hallway and into a classroom doorway.

When I got to the classroom, I found the door open, which sometimes happened if the custodians had been cleaning the floors and wanted them to dry before classes started the next day. I checked the floor. It was dry. I turned the lights on and saw that I'd entered a Geography class. To generate interest, the teacher had stuffed animals on top of all the shelves. I mean taxidermied items: a fox, a duck, a goose, that kind of thing. There was a closet, several shelves, and an open prep-room behind the class, so there were any number of places the squirrel could be hiding. I stood silently for a couple minutes, but there was no sound of scampering. I also noted that one of the ceiling tiles was missing in the corner of the room.

I didn't look very hard for Mr. Squirrel. One thing I didn't need on a Saturday morning, when I was by myself, was to have a frightened squirrel leap from a book shelf at me.

The T wing being the newest part of the school, only thirty years old at the time, there was supposed to be a pretty decent HVAC system, so it had very small windows that tilted on a hinge. In order to stay open, they needed to be wedged open with, say, a teacher's stapler, which is what I did. I then left a note on the board explaining that I'd wedged the window open, hoping Mr. Squirrel would leave of his own accord over the next couple of days. I really hoped that he hadn't planned on making the T wing his winter home that year. I also really hoped that the *one* squirrel would leave, rather than inviting a number of his friends over. Anyway, on Monday, the teacher and I went into her room before school started. We saw no evidence of a squirrel or squirrels, which I knew didn't mean any-thing, but we also saw that the window was shut and the stapler was nowhere to be found.

"I'll bet the squirrel knocked it loose when it left." she reasoned. "I'll check outside for it. It's probably laying in the grass right outside this window."

"No. You get set up for the day. I'll go check."

In seventeen years, I was never able to figure out the schedule for grass cutting at any of my schools. It seemed haphazard at best, but they always got it cut at my request for outdoor events, so I never complained, and I never really bothered to ask anyone how it was decided. I never would have guessed that they would have chosen that morning to cut the lawn, and that they'd start their work outside of the T wing with a stapler lying in the grass.

There were only three fairly recognizable but jagged pieces of the stapler left when I got outside the T wing window. Laughing, I brought them up to the teacher. "On the plus side, it looks like you were right about the squirrel knocking it loose. And also on the plus side, you get my brand new stapler."

And so, we thought, the episode of Mr. or Mrs. Squirrel was over.

We were wrong.

Later that day, I was called to a different classroom in the T wing a bit further up the hall. As I walked, in the teacher said, "Okay class. Silence please." Everyone became silent, and before I could ask why everyone was being so quiet I heard and understood. Something was scampering across the ceiling tiles above us.

"What do you think it is, Mr. Garlick?"

"I'm pretty sure it's the T wing Squirrel. I was hoping he'd left."

"My dad says squirrels carry disease!" "Squirrels are cute!""Is he trapped up there? Is he gonna die up there?" "What do they eat? Should we bring it food? Maybe nuts or bread?"

"No. It's not trapped. It got up there, right? And no, we're not going to feed it. We want it to leave. But I think it would be a good idea to leave your ceiling tiles in place, just so he doesn't join you during class."

For the next few days, the squirrel was heard above the ceiling tiles in different parts of the school. He got around. Then, on Thursday, there were no reports of squirrels in the ceiling. None on Friday either, but to be fair, I didn't pay any attention on Friday, because on Friday I had to deal with bats.

"I don't want to alarm anyone, but there's a bat hanging outside my classroom. He's okay where he is right now, but when the lunch bell rings and there are hundreds of kids in the hall, he's bound to wake up and then there'll be chaos." I was glad that it was a calm and reasonable teacher who noticed this, and not someone who would go crazy at the sight of a bat hanging outside their classroom door.

So the principal and I went upstairs with a ladder and a box and a piece of bristol board. We placed the box over the bat and slid the piece of bristol board between the ceiling and the box, dropping the until-then-sleeping bat into the box. We then took it outside and released it.

For some reason, we had to deal with two such episodes that fall, although I'd never heard of a bat being in the school before that and haven't since.

So a squirrel and a bat in one week, Saturday to Friday.

The following Monday, I was called to the auditorium because of the faint smell of natural gas. "I don't think it's a gas leak or anything," said the Drama teacher, "but it's not very pleasant for the class."

I walked through the auditorium. There was a faint odor of natural gas, a bit stronger by the stage. And so I went to see Elver about it.

"Do we have schematics for the school? The science labs all have natural gas on the third floor. Do the gas pipes run up through the auditorium? Maybe we damaged something moving all that stuff from Lowe when it closed, shoving it all up onto the stage."

We'd just moved from Lowe to Forster, and any "stuff" we couldn't find a place for quickly was shoved up onto the stage. We promised the Drama teacher we'd deal with it as quickly as possible, but asked her to leave the stage curtains closed until we could.

Well, we didn't have schematics, so Elver and I quietly went up onto the stage, trying very hard to be quiet and not interrupt the ESL Drama class going on in the auditorium. We tried, in the near-darkness, to determine if there was a gas leak and where it might be coming from, while also trying really hard not to bark our shins on whatever was lying about on the stage floor. There was a rack of graduation gowns on wheels, and when I moved it aside, I kicked one of the gowns that had apparently fallen off. I picked it up and felt that it had been tied in knots, and that it was kind of... moist... I didn't want to think why, and brought it to the front of the stage to get a better look. I parted the curtains, and looked down to see—"HOLY SHIT! THERE'S A DEAD SQUIRREL IN MY HAND!" I then dropped it like a hot potato.

I don't know whether I really shouted, "Holy shit!" I could have. I may have just shouted, "Geez!" Both are possible. I do know that the class found this hilarious! The first person they saw on Forster's stage was the vice-principal. It was a comedy routine: him and a dead squirrel. In any case, no one complained that I'd sworn. And two mysteries were solved that day: the Mystery of the Fate of the T-Wing Squirrel and the Mysterious Almost Gas Leak.

Wallace and the Coffee Can of Snakes

Just before the start of the school day, the VP and I were called to the third floor outside the science classes. There was a bit of a panic taking place. Teachers had caught two or three garter snakes in the halls and kids were screaming as the teachers walked by them to take the creatures outside.

A student took the VP, Scott Braithwaite, aside and said, "It was Wallace, Sir. He had a coffee can filled with them." So we had Wallace called to the office. As he walked in, he almost shouted, "I swear to God! I did not know there were snakes in that can!"

"Explain then, Wallace."

"Can I sit down? Okay. So. I'm walking to school this morning, minding my own business, when this kid comes up to me and says, 'Hey, watch this can of snakes for me until after school.' So he gives me the can and he walks away."

"You just said you didn't know there were snakes in there."

"I didn't! I mean, who goes around with a can of snakes? And who just gives it away? Why would someone have a bucket of snakes?"

"What did you think was in the can?"

"I didn't know, Sir! It was a coffee can. I thought maybe coffee. And then when I got to my locker, I thought, I wonder if it *is* a bucket of snakes. So I held it up to my face, and lifted the lid just a little, to peak in and holy! There were snakes! I dropped the can and ran!"

"Wallace, you know there are cameras in that hall, right? We can check out your story. It'll just take a couple minutes."

"That's what I'm hoping, Sir. I don't want to get suspended for bringing a bucket of snakes into the school!"

So Wallace took a seat in our send-out room while Scott used our video system to find the moments leading up to the Snake Panic, the moment of surprise, the dropping of the can (which was very reminiscent of me with the dead squirrel in my hand), and Wallace running off, leaving his locker wide open. After we stopped laughing—and showed the attendance secretary, so she could laugh—and then showed the teacher supervising the send-out room, so she could laugh too—we let Wallace go back to class.

And before you ask, no, we never did find out who gave Wallace the coffee can of snakes. Although we were fairly sure there were a lot more snakes than just the three caught by the teachers before school, we never did see another snake in the school.

The Puppy

"Mr. Garlick! We found a puppy outside! He was all alone! No mom or dad dog around! If we just left him out there he would have been hit by a car for sure! We've got him here in this box! Can we keep him here in your office until the end of the school day?"

This question was asked by two of the… neediest kids in the school, Kristin and James. By needy, I don't mean to imply they were poor, or that they weren't very bright. They both came from what you'd call "good homes," and from everything that I knew, they were loved by their parents. But they constantly needed attention from some-body—anybody really—from their peers, their teachers, the Child and Youth worker, or me.

At home, it was their parents, but once they were at school, it was one or more of us.

They were in grade nine and came from two different schools and two different neighbourhoods, but within two weeks, they found each other and began seeking attention together. I wouldn't have been *too* surprised to find out that they'd stolen the dog together. Or bought it and brought it to school just to make me deal with it.

"We brought it to the CYW first, Sir, but he said we should probably bring it to you and that you'd know what to do."

"Did he?" I made a mental note to have a talk to the Child and Youth worker about that later.

"Yes! We can't bring it from class to class all day. And we can't just bring it back outside and let it go. It'll just wander into the street and get itself killed!" Kristin looked like she was just about to start crying.

I looked into the box. He was a little, tawny coloured pup. Big paws. Nice markings. Maybe five or six weeks old. Cute. Couldn't really tell what breed; Lab type. Was going to be pretty big.

"My parents'll probably let me keep it if I bring it home after school." said James.

"And if yours won't, mine probably will..."

I looked at the clock; It was ten minutes after nine. School had just started, but they'd sought my attention out of ten minutes of class already.

"Well, then. Let's just call them and get that part of things settled first, okay?"

"Oh... On second thought, my parents probably won't let me keep it. Dad's 'lergic."

"Mine won't either... I've been asking for a dog for years..."

"Hmmm, tell you what. Let's call the Humane Society. I'm sure they would take this dog that you saved."

"Saved?"

"Sure! If you hadn't rescued it, like you said, it would probably have been hit right out front of the school. So let's get it saved permanently."

And so I called the Humane Society and put the phone on speaker phone.

"Hi. My name is Dave Garlick and I'm the vice-principal of Lowe Secondary School. I've got you on speaker phone and I'm sitting across from two young students and a stray puppy that they rescued this morning, no collar, no tags. I assured them that you'd send someone over here to pick it up and find it a forever home. That's right, isn't it?"

I didn't let them talk until I'd made my pitch and let them know that two impressionable young kids were listening in. I hoped I'd sold things pretty well.

I had.

"We'll send someone over straight away, Sir."

I thanked them and hung up the phone. The three of us were all smiles. "Now, I'll watch the pup until the Society gets here, okay? And you two can get to class." I looked up at my clock.

9:15 a.m.

We walked from my office into the main office. James announced to everyone there, "The three of us rescued a puppy today! The Humane Society is on the way to come pick it up and they said they'd find it a forever home!"

And then Beth Mueller, a teacher with a heart of gold who knew nothing of James and Kristin, their neediness, or how *lucky* I'd been to solve this situation in just over ten minutes with no tears, or how they were both off to class, feeling like heroes, cried out, "Not the Humane Society! They'll just put it to sleep!"

Hoping my voice didn't reflect the desperation I felt, I looked at Kristin—who once again seemed like she was going to cry—and then at Mrs. Mueller—hoping she'd understand what my eyes were trying to convey— and said, "No. No, Mrs. Mueller. Not little cute puppies like this one. Here, have a look. They'll take this puppy, which I'll watch in my office until the Society gets here, while Kristin and James go to class, and they'll find it a forever home. James and Kristin saved this puppy this morning, right?"

"Oh… It's a puppy… I thought… you were talking about an old… sick… dog. Yes, I'm sure they'll find this one a forever home."

"Thanks, Mrs. Mueller. Now, you two, off to class." We watched them leave.

"You know, Dave, if they don't find a home for that pup, or it turns out to be sick, they may end up putting it to sleep."

"Well, I guess we have to hope they find a home for it then."

One week later, Beth Mueller walked into my office with a Polaroid picture of a very familiar-looking puppy. Beth had been to the Humane Society three times between our in-school incident and that morning.

"I've just been approved to adopt her. She's been given her shots, de-wormed, and given a clean bill of health. I'm going to call her Lowe-la. Get it? I get to provide her with her forever home!"

"Beth, are you sure you want to do this?"

"Well, I couldn't let our new VP be made a liar, could I? And Dave, she's very cute."

Kids

Mrs. Mavis Patchoulol, my Science head, (whose name was sometimes mistaken for "Mrs. Pudgy Girl" by elementary students visiting the school), called me on my cell phone one afternoon to say, "Dave, if you want to come up now you can, they're gone."

"Mavis, why are you calling me on my cell phone? Who's gone?"

"So no one told you. Good. I asked them not to. Said it might get you in trouble."

"Mavis, what are you talking about?"

"It's okay. You can come up now. Come to the science prep room."

So I went upstairs to the science prep room. As I walked in, Mavis handed me a small shooter glass. "It's a chocolate martini. If you find it too sweet, I've got brandy as well. I only bring it on special occasions and I only share it with people if I know they won't mind. *You* don't mind, do you? And I won't even tell you it's a special-occasion day until the end of the day, so you don't have to worry about it all day."

I thought back to my early career, and how much times had changed in thirty years. When I started teaching, the staff rooms were *all* smoking areas. Some teachers smoked in their prep rooms. Dave Sartorin and Dino Tarantola smoked cigars in their prep rooms. And when I was a student, not much farther back, teachers and students drank together in the Dominion House and Sid's Bridge House after school. Now, a very small minority of teachers smoked at all, and none at school. Drinking only happened off-site, and never with students around.

"No, I don't mind. Thanks."

We sat quietly for a few minutes, talking about the semester so far, and how Mavis was seriously beginning to think about retiring, maybe even by the end of the year. She was happy with the department she'd built to that point, and was confident that one of the young teachers would step up and take over. Mavis would then get to devote more time to her hobby farm.

"Oh!" I exclaimed, remembering her phone call. "When you called me a few minutes ago, you said it was safe to come up, because they'd gone. Which teachers were you talking about?"

"Teachers? No, I wasn't talking about any of them. All the teachers up here are fine with this."

"Oh. So you were talking about the kids."

"Yes…" And then she started laughing. Laughing so hard that, for a while, she couldn't talk.

I thought she must have a great story for me. "What's so funny?"

"You guessed it! The special occasion today was that I brought in two of my young goats—*kids*—from home! I showed the students how we draw blood from them for testing. My husband came to pick them up after school. I told the students not to tell *anyone* because you'd get in trouble if anyone found out. They kept the secret all day long!"

Mice

Every school has mice—well, I don't actually *know* that *every* school has mice. Every school I ever worked in had mice. In the city, I always worked in older buildings, all coming up on a hundred years old. In the county, my school, Western, was literally surrounded by corn fields. Weirdly, at the city schools, Forster, Lowe and Walkerville, people just accepted that there would be mice. They wanted them caught, but they knew they'd be there every fall as it got colder outside. At Western, in the middle of the county, *I* expected mice, but the parents, who all lived on country roads or in small towns and villages, *they* were shocked.

I received calls of complaint every year. "My son tells me he's seen mouse traps in the school!"

"Yes. It's October and there's a chill in the air. When it gets cold, the mice in the fields want to find somewhere warm. We're it."

"But you're going to catch them all, right?"

"We're certainly going to try."

"Mr. Garlick, I'm going to call back in early December. I want you to be able to tell me you've caught them all, okay?"

"Okay... How will I know?"

"What?"

"How will I know that I've caught them all?"

Silence. "Have a nice day, Mr. Garlick."

This next part will seem like it has nothing to do with mice, but it will. Trust me.

I received a phone call from a person in the community who thought she was helping me. She'd been to the hairdresser and overheard a conversation between two other clients, and no, she didn't know who they were. They were talking and apparently there was a boy named Jordan who maybe was going to bring a gun to school on Wednesday and her appointment had been on Monday, and she'd thought and thought about it, and well, today was Wednesday and she thought she'd better call...

Principals get paid to think about worst-case scenarios and how to avoid them. *Probably* the lady was just a well-meaning crazy person. Or *probably* she'd misheard the conversation and Jordan was going to bring a bundt to school today. If that was the case, then ignoring the phone call would lead to nothing. But maybe... A quick search showed me we had five Jordans at Western and that, luckily, two were away that day.

I called my VP, Hazel Keefner, into my office. I made her aware of the situation, gave her two lockers and lock combinations to look into, and asked her to humour me.

"Better safe than sorry, I guess," she said as she left.

There was nothing in the locker I checked, and nothing in the first locker that Hazel looked through. But her second locker wouldn't open. "Great. So we're going to have to get Jordan to open it." Hazel said.

"What do we tell him? That a crazy lady called to accuse maybe him of bringing a gun to school? But we have to check just to make sure the lady is crazy and there isn't a gun in there?"

"Hmmm. No. Jordan can sometimes be a little... dramatic. Fragile. It might just send him into a funk. I know! We'll tell him we saw a mouse go into his locker!"

So we called Jordan out of class to his locker.

"Jordan," I said, pointing at the locker, "Is this your locker?"

"No Sir. *This* is my locker," he said, pointing to one which was two lockers away.

"Oh!" said Hazel. "Because we saw a mouse go into *that* locker!" pointing at the one that Jordan had just said was his.

"That's awful! I hate mice! In fact, the whole reason I have *that* locker, is that when Mrs. Seguin assigned me *this* locker," gesturing to the one I had pointed at, "there was mouse poop on the shelf, so she told me I could have this one instead.

Would one of you two mind searching it for me? I don't want a mouse jumping out at me."

So Hazel opened the locker and searched it. And while there was no gun, there *was* a mouse, which jumped out when Hazel opened the locker.

After Jordan stopped screaming—which, really, only lasted a second or two—he thanked us. "Thanks Mrs. Keefner. Thanks Mr. Garlick. That would have been a shock. I hate mice!"

Another Mouse

This story actually has very little to do with me.

Vice-Principal Norm Ross was standing by the back door to the school, greeting kids as they arrived at the building. Close to 100 percent of the kids were bussed to the school, so as the buses dropped kids off, Norm was there to give them a fist bump or shake their hands. He thought it was a nice way for the kids to start the day.

Also, it had snowed the night before, and this was a way to make sure that the kids weren't throwing snowballs at the buses or trying to bring snow into the school.

"Mason! Drop the snow!" Norm would say, pointing his finger like it was a gun at Mason. And Mason would drop the snow.

But there were forty kids on each bus, so when three buses arrived at the same time, it was difficult to watch all the kids at the same time. Norm turned just in time to see Jeremy Foulds throw *something* onto the roof, and he heard a gentle *plop* above him.

"Mr. Foulds. You didn't throw a snowball onto the roof, did you?"

Righteous indignation. Quick, quick anger. "WHY WOULD YOU ACCUSE ME OF THROWING A SNOWBALL ON THE ROOF? I DID NOT THROW A SNOWBALL ON THE ROOF! CHECK THE CAMERAS! I'LL BET YOU A BILLION DOLLARS I DIDN'T THROW A SNOWBALL ON THE ROOF!"

Mid-term exams were starting that day, and Norm thought it best to let things go. No harm done: calm the kid down and let him write his exam. "Sorry, Jeremy. I must be mistaken. Good luck on your exam, okay? You've got this!"

He offered Jeremy a fist bump, and almost as quickly as he'd gotten angry he calmed down. "Thanks, Mr. Ross. I'm a bit on edge, I guess. Math exam today,"

"You'll do fine."

The kids all wrote their exams. and the buses returned to pick up the kids and bring them home. Norm and I were at the back door to say good-bye to the kids as they left. Norm saw Jeremy walking towards him with a big smile. "I think I aced it, Sir!"

Norm smiled back and said, "I've got to know... I saw you throw *something* onto the roof. If it wasn't a snowball, what was it?"

The smile vanished. Not anger now, but sheepishness. And quiet. "Mouse."

"You threw a mouse onto the roof?"

"I caught it in my room this morning. I thought this place would be a nice, warm spot for it!"

"Wait, you threw a mouse onto the roof? A live mouse?

"Well, it was alive when I caught it..."

Big Birds.

Very occasionally, at every school I worked in, a small bird would get into the school, a sparrow or a starling. They generated a bit of chaos and poop, but they never really wanted to stay, and all you had to do was open the door or the classroom window they had flown in through, and they'd leave.

We never had any *big* birds make their way into the school, but one morning, my Learning Support teacher, Annie Bondy, said to me in the staff room, "Mr. Garlick, there's a wild turkey in our parking lot and I think it's injured." Annie was one of several animal lovers on staff. She arranged for the "Kiss a Pig" event each year, and the "Kiss the Mystery Animal" event. The mystery animal turned out to be a baby lion.

"Why do you think it's injured?" I asked.

"Well, I had to drive around it. It's just sitting in the parking lot."

"Maybe it's tired. Or bull-headed."

"I'm pretty sure they're a protected species..." This was Gary Edwards, a Math teacher.

"And what does that mean to me?"

"Well, maybe we should protect it from the kids."

Our chef and cooking teacher, who preferred to be called "Chef," said, "*I'm* pretty sure they're delicious!

Dave, if you kill it, I'll cook it up for us. I can make it lunch for about ten of us! And then I'll make turkey soup for tomorrow!"

"Chef!" this was Annie Bondy, appalled; Chef laughed.

This all took place between about seven and seven-thirty in the morning, when all the teachers would be at school but the kids were just starting to arrive. Over the walkie-talkie, I heard, "Mr. Garlick, kids are coming into the main office telling us there's a big bird in the parking lot. It may be a buzzard or an eagle, but the kids say it's a turkey."

So I called E.R.C.A., the Essex Region Conservation Authority. "If it is a turkey, it's not a protected species. If I were you, I'd just chase it away with a broom. If it *is* injured that won't work, and you'll know right away." The worker from E.R.C.A. advised me.

I grabbed a broom and headed to the back of the school, where I was met by Annie, Gary and Chef. "It's definitely a turkey, Dave." "And it's definitely delicious. Well, it would be…"

Two students walked up behind us. "Oh! So you heard about the turkey. Sir, if you give us the broom, we'll chase it away. That's what you're supposed to do."

Sometimes, kids know best.

Who Does this Guy Look Like?

This short story is almost entirely true. I've changed the retired bishop's name, but very little else. It's basically an anecdote to tell the reader about Western Secondary School, which was the first school at which I was the principal. Western is my Board's vocational school in the county. Every student has to have at least one learning disability in order to apply to attend there. Most have multiple learning disabilities, and while that can lead to some challenges, it can also lead to the occasional miracle. This anecdote does not contain any miracles, really, but it does do a good job of telling you the kind of "good works" that happen there all the time.

It's not every day that you meet a Roman Catholic bishop. In fact, for me, there was only one day that I met a Roman Catholic bishop.

Bishop Armand LaBrecque (ret.)

I'm not Catholic. I'm not particularly religious; I'm not what you'd even call a "regular church goer," unless by "regular" you'd mean for weddings and funerals and such.

So, really, there aren't many opportunities for me to meet a bishop.

But in the third year of my principalship at Western Secondary School, Bishop Armand LaBrecque (ret.) presented himself, with his calling card, to our main office and offered us his services as a volunteer.

"Since I moved back to Essex County, I've heard all about your fine institution, and the good works you do, and I'd like to help. I'm retired now, so I have time to give you."

"Well, thank you very much… I'm sorry, do I call you 'Your Eminence?'"

"Not necessary, young man. I'm retired. Please, just call me Armand."

"Well, thank you very much, Armand!"

"Yes. I've heard how you work with troubled youth and you do handicraft with them."

"I'm sorry?"

"Handicraft. You know, painting balsa wood, putting plaster of Paris on balloons. That kind of thing. I can help with that."

"I'm sorry, Armand. I think you've been given the wrong impression of our school. We're a regular high school, except every one of our students has at least one learning disability. We teach them how best to learn in spite of their disability and the vast majority graduate from high school with experience in a trade. May I offer you a tour?"

And so I gave Bishop Armand LaBrecque (ret.) the same tour I gave prospective students and their families forty or fifty times a year. He saw our library, complete with students reading, writing, and working on computers; computer labs, science labs, our art room; and our regular classrooms, with students learning History, English, and Math. And then he saw our technical wing—the greenhouse, woodshop, autoshop, small engine shop, autobody shop, metal shop and welding booths, followed by the gymnasium—and he was very apologetic. To this point, at every stop he'd simply said, "Oh my!"

"I'm very sorry, Mr. Garlick. You *are* doing good works here, but not of the type I was led to believe. This school is amazing!"

"Thank you, Bishop. We all like the place. Of course, you're still welcome to volunteer, but I think the work would be different than you'd thought."

"I'll have to give it some serious thought…"

"But we're not finished! In some ways, I've saved the best for last!"

"I can't imagine…"

"Close your eyes as we turn this corner."

We were now at my favourite part of the school, smell-wise. While fresh-cut wood holds a special place in my heart, there's not much that bests the smell of fresh-baked bread.

"Oh my!" he said as we turned the corner and entered the foods hall.

Armand got to see the bake shop in high gear. Kids were making the bread and buns that would be served that day at lunch and then sold to the staff and any students that wanted to purchase a fresh loaf of bread for a dollar at the end of the day. Larry Baker (his real name) was very proud to show off his class room.

"We make hot cross buns for Easter, and paczkis for Shrove Tuesday. We make wedding cakes, cakes of all kinds, and pies. Many kinds of bread. May I offer you a loaf? Free to bishops today! I insist!" As he said this, he gave the bishop a freshly baked loaf of white bread and a bag of buns. "The buns are crusty. The ones you have in some restaurants that are so soft? They're incredibly high in fat. These are much more healthy for you."

I was incredibly proud of the whole school to this point of the tour. The teachers had all been eager to show off their classrooms and shops and the kids had all been very respectful and polite. "Good morning, Sir. Hope you're having a good day!" and "It feels just like spring out there today, doesn't it, Sir?"

Our students were not known for their social skills, but to this point, they'd been *better* than the kids I'd worked with in my previous schools. No one except for Larry Baker had even mentioned religion after I'd introduced the bishop in the different classes. And Larry's references were perfect, as we were just coming up on Easter.

Next, I took Bishop LaBrecque to our kitchen, where students were busy making lunch for almost 600 students and fifty staff, as they did five days a week. Chefs Carl and Roz were just as proud as Larry to show off their students.

"We teach the students to make over 100 different kinds of soup every year! In addition to the typical fare you see at other schools—hamburgers, tacos, fries, pizza—we serve three different entrées each day to anyone who wants them. I'm told our food is better than most restaurants in our county!"

I told the Bishop, "My first day here, they served chicken cordon bleu with asparagus spears and potatoes Parisienne for four dollars and fifty cents, with soup and fresh bread for an extra dollar-fifty! I gained eighteen pounds my first semester until I learned to control myself. It's hard working at one of the best restaurants in Windsor-Essex, when they deliver the food right to your desk!"

We laughed and once again, Bishop LaBrecqe said, "Oh my!"

The last remaining stop was our school's restaurant, which effectively taught students how to run a high-class restaurant, every day. They prepared the menus, set the tables, waited on the customers, served as many as forty customers from the staff and community in forty-five minutes, took their money at the end of their "shift," and then cleaned up and prepped for the next day.

When the Bishop and I walked in, five senior boys were just finishing setting the tables and placing menus at each place setting.

"Men? I'm just finishing up a tour and this is our last stop. I'd like you to meet Bishop LaBrecque."

All five stopped what they were doing and came over to shake the bishop's hand. They were clearly impressed. "I've never met a real bishop before. I can't wait to tell my parents!"

Without meaning to, they'd lined themselves up in a row and were looking at the bishop, not sure what to do at this point. Would it be impolite to simply turn and go back to work? They looked at each other and realized that, in their minds, a rather special student was in their group.

"Should we tell him?" "What do you think?" "No." "Yes!" "Let's tell him!"

To this point, as I said, I'd been incredibly proud of the kids. But I had no idea what they were going to tell the bishop. Still, they'd left me little choice, as we'd both just heard their conversation.

"Tell us… what?" I asked.

They grabbed the boy in the middle and pushed him toward the bishop and me.

"Who does this kid look like?" they asked. "He looks like someone famous! Who's he look like?"

The Bishop and I exchanged confused looks. Although most people bear *some* resemblance to *somebody* you might know, somebody famous, this kid just looked like a kid. And who would these students think that both I and the bishop would recognize in this young man?

"I'm sorry, I don't know. Who does he look like?" asked the bishop.

"He looks just like Jesus!"

Again, still, the young man looked like, well, a young man—no more or less like Jesus than I did. And I, at least, had a beard.

The bishop and I looked at each other again, and still looked confused.

The boys looked at each other and their young friend and realized why we were confused.

"Oh! We forgot! He cut his hair and shaved off his beard and moustache last week. But when he grows his hair long and has a beard and moustache, he looks just like Jesus!"

Once again, the bishop said, "Oh my!"

Flame and Chopper

"My father's coming to see you today, and he's mad!"

"Really! What's he mad about?"

"He's mad at you!"

"Well I guess I'd better talk to him then, eh?"

When the student had left the office, my secretary told me that over the last couple years, the boy had threatened to have his angry father come in a few times, but no one had met this man yet. The boy threatened to have his dad come in whenever he was annoyed, usually at the principal. The father was a member of a biker gang and went by the nickname of 'Chopper.' He asked for mail from the school to be addressed to 'Chopper.'

"If he's really coming today, maybe we should have the police here, you know, just in case," said my head secretary.

"Because a parent may or may not be coming because he may or may not be angry at me? Seems excessive, don't you think?"

"I suppose…… Say, how do you think someone gets a nickname like that?"

I could think of a few ways, none of them good, some involving tire irons or baseball bats. But I still didn't change my mind.

Chopper did stop by that day. I forget what he was supposed to be angry about. He turned out to be very polite. We had a great conversation about his son. We agreed that he had all kinds of potential and that maybe he was old enough to stop threatening other kids and the principal with his dad. That that was something you might expect from a student in grade school, not one in grade ten. Chopper had a cup of coffee with me; and we laughed and had a great visit.

As he rose to leave, I asked him, because I felt I had to, "I'm sorry, Sir, but I have to ask you, how did you get your nickname?"

"We all get nicknames. I got mine because of my size. I'm just five foot one, you know."

"Really? I hadn't noticed." (I had) He was, for a biker, objectively cute, almost cuddly. It was an effort not to pinch his cheek. Still, I wouldn't have wanted him to be really angry with me.

I only met one other biker in my time at Western, although there was a 'clubhouse' just up the street, and a few of our students had bikers for parents. That one other biker earned me some 'street cred' with the kids and the staff. Mrs. Parent, our attendance secretary, had warned me that 'Flame' St. Amour was coming to see me, and was concerned that I didn't seem as concerned as she was. She let a few teachers know, and I didn't find out why they were all in the foyer with me at lunch until later.

I was talking with them and some kids in the foyer of the school when a decidedly un-cute biker came in the front door. Chopper had been a bit of a bust, from a fear-inducing perspective, but Flame held much more promise. At six foot four, he was tall and muscular, sporting a full, black beard with streaks of grey, Elvis Costello glasses, and a bandana. He wore a bit of a scowl as his eyes adjusted to the light in the foyer. Then he saw me and the scowl turned into a charming smile. "Garlick! It *is* you! My kid told me there was a Garlick Principal here, but I didn't think it'd be you! You still got your bike?"

"Michael! How the heck are you?"

"Not too bad." He waved the cane. "I'm gonna need this until I have a second surgery on my back, but I can't complain. Not bad for an old guy."

He came over and gave me a bear hug

"Come on in! Can I offer you a coffee?" I asked when he put me down.

"Never touch the stuff. Can I bother you for a cool glass of water?"

Michael 'Flame' St. Amour and I grew up together, one street apart. His mother was my first Band instructor and taught me how to play the saxophone. We lost touch when he moved away from Windsor to the county. Michael had grown up and joined a biker gang, but always seemed a decent sort.

I forget why he visited, but, like Chopper, I had to ask him about his nickname.

"Flame? I earned that name a long time ago. Slid off the back of my bike doing sixty. I had metal heels and toes on my boots and metal studs just about everywhere else. I sent up a rooster tail of sparks for a couple hundred yards and from then on, everyone's called me Flame."

Things aren't always as you imagine they'll be. Chopper and Flame taught me that.

The Golf Hole and Sixty Trees

"You know, Dave, there are a lot of jobs in golf course maintenance." This was Jordan Butler, one of the Horticulture teachers at Western Secondary School. "It's true! Entry level, summer jobs, full time, jobs that you can stay in, make into a career! Greens-keepers make very good money, do very well for themselves."

"Are you talking about co-op positions?" These were jobs that students held during the school year. Kids would be taken on as a sort of apprentice, get special training, and earn credits towards their diploma. The big advantage for the employer was that they would get a young person with an interest in working for them, but wouldn't have to pay them. If the kid did really well, sometimes that co-op position turned into a part time job, a summer job, or even a career.

"Yes. Those too. A lot of the area courses would be happy to take on one of my—our—kids."

"What do you need me to do for you?"

"For co-op positions? Nothing. I'll talk to Tory Prince," who was the Co-op teacher, "and I've got connections at a lot of the courses. I'll call them."

"Well, *what* then?"

He leaned forward in his chair, resting his forearms on my desk. "Here's what I was thinking. We build a golf hole! No! Hear me out! It'll be good!"

He hadn't given me time to react when he said, "No! Hear me out!" I smiled and realized he'd practised this a few times before coming to me with the presentation. It was important to him.

"I'll teach the kids the mechanics behind a golf hole. The difference between the grass on the fairway, and the grass on a green. How to prepare the soil, the kind of seed you use, and the techniques to maintain them. And then they'll actually get to do it! We've got enough empty land out there to build, what, three, four golf holes! We could do something new every year for the rest of my career! Golf courses would chase our kids down with that kind of experience! They'll have jobs—good jobs, mind you— before they even leave high school!"

"You've sold me. I'm in."

"You don't have to answer right now, just—what?"

"I'm in. It's a great idea."

"Really?"

"Sure. I just need to get permission from downtown. That shouldn't be hard."

"Really?"

"Yup. Before I leave this evening, I'll send Alvin Carsten an email. Mr. Carsten is the superintendent in charge of facilities. He might even want to supply us with some of the specialized equipment necessary. I'll let you know when his answer is an excited "yes" and we can get started.

"Really?"

"Yes! Great idea, Jordan! Good on you!"

He left my office a little shell-shocked, not expecting it to be such an easy sell. But I was all about "real life" experiences for our kids, and securing good jobs after they left us. Most of the kids at Western never went to college. High school was all they got. And good jobs for kids with learning disabilities are always at a premium.

Jordan stuck his head back into my office. "I should have mentioned another part of my idea. Staff get to play for free after school. Great practice!"

I smiled. "Nope. Fifty cents a hole. Or maybe a buck. Fundraiser. The money could go towards a scholarship for the kids. I'll chip in, pardon the pun, the first fifty bucks so everyone who wants to gets a free hole. We can have a "Closest to the Pin" night: five bucks to enter, the winner takes half the prize. Of course, most of us would be happy just to win our five bucks back and get a small trophy or something. A hole-in-one gets free lunch for a semester. There must be a dozen ways to have this pay for itself."

"Those are great ideas, Dave! Thanks!"

But none of that happened. I wrote my email to Mr. Carsten and made what I thought was an excellent pitch. Pushed hard on the idea of jobs for kids with learning disabilities and real world experience. I may have even given him naming rights. I wrote it up, read it over, and sent it off, confident in a speedy and excited approval.

But, again, none of that happened. Maybe I should have copied the request to the director, but I don't think that would have made a difference. The one thing Jordan had neglected to mention was that I wasn't the first principal the Golf Hole idea had been sold to, or even the second. I think I was the fourth. And we had all tried to sell it to Mr. Carsten, who'd been a superintendent that whole time.

So Alvin didn't answer my email in the affirmative. He didn't send me a response at all. He simply called me the next morning and "tore me a new one" for about ten minutes. He made sure I understood who was in charge of the school grounds and that there would never, *never* be a golf hole built on school board property. At least, not as long as he was a superintendent, and he didn't plan on retiring any time soon.

He finished his yelling episode with, "Listen, Mr. Garlick, spade one does not go in to the earth without my express, written permission." He spoke slowly, enunciating every syllable very clearly. "Do I have your understanding?"

"Yes, Sir."

I hung up the phone, about five seconds after he'd hung up on me.

That was the first, but not the last time I was chastised by a member of the senior admin team.

I gave Jordan the bad news, for some reason not blaming him for not giving me the whole story. Like me, he was just thinking about the kids.

"Thanks for trying, Dave."

About three days later, Martin Godwin came running into my office. "I just got off the phone with the local Conservation Authority! They're going to give us sixty trees!"

"That's great, Martin! For free?"

"Yep!" He sat down across from me. For just a second, I thought he was going to swing his feet up onto my desk. He seemed *that* proud.

"That's great! And how much do you think we can sell them for?" I asked.

"What?"

"How much do you want to sell them for? It'll be a fundraiser for the school, right?"

"Well, no. I thought we'd plant them around the perimeter of the property. Think of the oxygen they'll provide to the planet. I've been telling my kids about this for days. And they'll actually have the opportunity to plant them! They can't wait! Fifteen kids—four trees each! We can get it finished during class! You won't even have to bother another teacher!"

I don't know why I didn't say "No!" right away. I don't know why I didn't tell him he should have told me all about this before going to the Conservation Authority, and that I was sorry, but it just couldn't happen. Well, actually, yes, I do know. The truth was that Martin taught a small group of "intellectually challenged" kids and was doing a fine job. This was a great thing he'd planned. His kids would be excited and they'd tell their parents how much they enjoyed high school. Maybe in a couple weeks they'd be able to tell their parents how sad they were that their principal had been fired.

Maybe I was worrying over nothing. With a few days' lead time, I could write Alvin—no, *call* Alvin—and ask permission. I would sound servile. Apologetic. Push the "limited kids" thing. I just needed a few days lead time. Just a few days.

"So when are they dropping off the trees?" I asked, looking at the calendar, pretending it might run up against something in my busy schedule, something I'd have to put off or cancel. "Sorry, I can't attend the principals' meeting this month," I'd say. "I have to plant some trees with a class!"

"That's the best part! Tomorrow! And they'll even help us place them so they don't interfere with the soccer pitch or any over head wires!"

I didn't step on Martin for this. Didn't tell him that maybe I'd get fired over it. The fact was, I didn't want to step on him. And as I write this, I'm proud to say that I can't recall once in fourteen years when I *did* step on a teacher's idea. My job was to say "Yes" as often as I could. "Yes" and "How can I help?" or "Yes" and just get out of the way.

So I didn't call the Conservation Authority behind Martin's back and beg for a few extra days or weeks. I didn't ask for a reprieve. I just made sure Martin had informed the parents. He had called them all and had signed parental consent forms. He'd also made sure there were enough gloves and shovels to go around.

I held my breath and hoped for the best.

The Authority arrived at seven the next morning, with sixty six-foot trees on a flatbed. They positioned the trees around the perimeter of the property with the help of Mr. Godwin, who acted like a kid at Christmas the whole time .

"These trees are all indigenous, Dave! They'll grow really well here! In a few years, the kids'll be able to picnic under them. And in a few more, they'll be able to bring their kids here and tell them about the day they planted them!"

I actually began to feel good about this project. We were helping out the environment and teaching our kids how to plant trees. I knew people who got really good summer jobs planting trees up north; maybe some of these kids would be doing that in a couple-few years! And most importantly, maybe I wouldn't get fired.

"We'll plant them all in period one. Will you come and watch, Dave? I told the kids you might."

"Sure!" But in the back of my head I heard Alvin Carsten, senior superintendent—"Spade one doesn't go into the earth without…"

I went into my office, closed the door, and drank a cup of coffee. *Maybe I won't get fired*, I thought. *Maybe I'll just get a letter in my file. Maybe I'll just get reamed again. Maybe it'll just be a suspension…* I had no idea.

And maybe, I thought, *maybe he won't even find out! I mean, how's he going to know? It's not like he comes out here ever. Who's going to tell him? Not me!*

Dave, you're worrying about nothing!

So I went out after the opening bell and the national anthem. I walked around the property Good on You-ing the kids, clapping Martin on the back, and thanking the Conservation Authority reps for coming. I even thanked the man who was taking pictures for them.

"Oh, I'm not from the Authority. I'm Mike Branson from your local newspaper."

At this, Martin Godwin came over. "Yeah, I'm sorry Dave. I tried to get the CBC to come. Thought it'd be good for the kids to see themselves on TV. But the newspaper is pretty good! The kids can cut the pictures out and save them. I'll post a few on the bulletin board outside my room. Maybe you can put one in the newsletter you send out to parents and downtown! "Say, Mr. Branson, how many people read the paper, anyway?"

I'd forgotten. Mr. Godwin was from out of town and new to our community. He didn't know the answer. But I did.

"Just about everyone reads it, Sir."

"Yes… Well… Good on you, Mr. Godwin. Thanks for coming, Mr. Branson."

And the next morning, at the bottom of the front page, yes, the very front page, was a picture of one of *my* students, jumping onto a spade, driving it into the earth. "Spade one…" At least my name wasn't mentioned.

I wish this story had a more, I don't know, conclusive ending than it actually does. I wasn't fired. I wasn't suspended. I didn't even get a letter in my file. In fact, Mr. Carsten never even mentioned the "Spade One" thing again, or the sixty trees. I never even found out why. Maybe he was one of the few who didn't read the paper. Or maybe the director saw the article first and liked the positive news story about the school. But for about a month, I waited to be fired, or at least suspended. Waited for the call from downtown telling me to come to the Board for a meeting.

But wouldn't a golf hole or two have been nice?

Terrence and His Mother's Wallet

My first vice-principal, Bradley Hooper, was older than I was. He'd been a VP for more than five years when I arrived at the school. Often, he said, "Nothing surprises me. I've seen it all."

When he said that around me, I'd say, "Brad?" and he would remember. "Well, except for that one time this year. *That* surprised me."

***

I took a call from Mrs. Harker at 7:00 a.m. one morning in February. The police had called me ten minutes earlier, so I was expecting her call.

"When my son gets to school this morning, would you please search his locker? I'm pretty certain he's stolen my wallet." The police had given me this same information and made the same request.

"He's not stupid enough to keep it on his person, so I'm pretty sure he'll stuff it in his locker. It doesn't look like anything a teenage boy should have. It's black eel skin.

If you find it, I just want it back, okay? I don't want him suspended or anything."

So at about 8:30, after school had started and I was sure the boy had come to school that day, the VP and I went to his locker and opened it. We keep a record of every student's locker combination, as well as the combination of every lock we buy for the school, so this part was usually pretty easy. Inside, we found five winter coats, and, on the locker shelf, a metal cigarette container with five joints in it.

"Aw, shoot. Now, even if we don't find the wallet we're going to have to suspend the kid…"

We went through the pockets of each coat, but found nothing. No wallet, no identification, nothing. And two of the coats were clearly girls coats.

We took the five winter coats and the container of marijuana and started back towards the office. As luck would have it, the student—I'll call him Terrence or Terry (not his real name, nor was his mother's name Harker) —was just coming out of the bathroom, right in front of us, and he was wearing a winter coat. "Hi Mr. Garlick! Hi Mr. Hooper! Do you want some help with all that stuff?" Cool as a cucumber, I thought.

"G'morning Terrence. No, that's okay. Would you mind coming with us to my office for a minute?"

"Sure! No problem! You're sure I can't help you?"

By this point, we were in the main office, walking down the hall towards my office. The VP and I put the five coats on my desk.

"Terry, would you close the door please?"

"Sure."

"Can you explain all this?"

"All what?" He seemed genuinely confused.

"These coats. They were all in your locker."

"*My* locker, Sir?"

"Yup."

"I don't really have a locker, Sir. I mean, you assigned me one back in September, and you gave me a lock, but I've never used it."

Now I was confused.

"So all this stuff was in there? Who does it belong to?" Terry asked.

"We were hoping you would tell us… By the way, do you have any idea why we might be looking into your locker?"

"Lemme guess. My mom told you to."

"Why would you say that?"

"This morning, I'm waiting for the bus, and my mom drives up in her pickup truck. Hair still in curlers. She starts yelling at me, just as the bus pulls up. Something about her wallet. So I just ignored her and got on the bus."

"So you didn't take her wallet."

"No!"

"Would you mind—"

Before I could finish the sentence, he started emptying his pockets. Pants first: *his* wallet, a lighter, a pack of cigarettes, some loose change. Then he moved to his winter coat: a tissue, a half-cigarette, a hacky sack (those were pretty big back then), but then he pulled out a clear plastic bag filled with what looked like more marijuana than I'd ever seen. He placed it on my desk along with everything else. It seemed to have no more importance to him than his lighter. Certainly, he didn't act as though he was putting an expulsion and probable jail time on my desk. There was *that* much in the bag.

"Uhh… Terry… What is that?"

"This?" He said, picking it back up. "This is my father's ashes. He died back in November, you know. I'm meeting my aunt for lunch today, and we're going to split them up. She wants some."

I looked closer, and it was indeed ashes. Not pot.

"Say, you wouldn't have an elastic band or something, would you? I'd hate for them to spill out into my pocket."

I gave him a handful of elastic bands while I quickly, mentally, went through all the regulations I could think of about carrying your father's ashes around in your pocket in a school. It was not something I'd encountered before. Or have encountered since, for that matter. It wasn't covered in principals' training. I certainly wasn't going to be suspending him for it.

"Can I go back to class, Sir?"

"Uh… Sure, Terrence…" But then I remembered. "Say, do you remember giving your locker combination to anyone? Maybe even back in September?"

He rubbed his chin, and looked at the ceiling, clearly trying to remember. "Let's see… Fuuuu (He lengthened the word out so much I'm not *sure* he ever really swore, but he probably did.) Oh yeah! Just one kid! Spencer!"

Terrence (again, not his real name) left my office and Brad and I looked at each other in disbelief. I don't remember if we laughed right then. We've laughed about it many times since.

I had Spencer called to the office. He walked in, took one look at my desk and said, with absolutely no prompting:

"You got me, Sir. The girls coats belong to Tiffany. The boys coats are all mine. She doesn't know anything about the pot you found on the shelf in that tin."

He was fine with the suspension. At eighteen, he was an adult. I didn't even have to call home. One of the easiest suspensions of my career. "And you know something, Sir? If I had just followed your advice and used my own locker, you never would have caught me."

About an hour later, Mrs. Harker called me back.

"You don't need to search my son's locker after all. I found my wallet. It was in my other coat pocket! Oh! Would you please remind Terry his aunt is taking him out to lunch today? He's going to share some of his father's ashes with her. It would be just like him to forget."

Sometimes—In Fact, Almost Always—They Grow Up

Mason Forget held the record for most suspensions from school.

Forty-four.

Forty-four suspensions from school in under four years.

Now, to be fair, I don't *know* that this was a real record. There may have been other kids suspended more often at other schools, or in different eras, but certainly he'd been suspended from school more often than any other student during my time as a principal. The suspensions were usually for goofy things: pouring a box of Cheerios into a toilet; putting three firecrackers into a waste bin in the hall; toilet-papering his teachers' cars and then posting pictures of himself doing it on Facebook.

That kind of thing.

There was the occasional fight, mostly in grade nine. But he was not a kid I worried about. Eventually, he would grow up, get a job, get married, and then karma would pay him back by giving him a child just like he'd been.

That's what I knew would happen. So I never worried about Mason Forget.

I did not anticipate him coming into my office after the most recent suspension, in February of his graduating year, to tell me that he was done.

"I'm done, Sir."

"Done what?"

"I'm done with being suspended. It's not going to happen again. No more high-school hijinks."

"Is your mother putting you up to this?"

"Nope. I'm just done. Time to grow up."

"Well good for you, Mason! I'm proud of you. But I've got to tell you; you're one kid I've never worried about. I just thought that this would happen a couple years after you finished school. I thought you'd end up getting fired from your first job after school and then you'd figure things out."

"Thanks, Sir. I guess. You won't be seeing me in here any more. You'll just see me in class or in the lunch room. No more suspensions for this guy."

And he was as good as his word. February finished. March came and went. Mason went into the month like a lamb and came out like a lamb. The teachers began to comment. "I didn't believe it when you told us, Dave. I felt sure that he was playing you somehow. But he's been good as gold."

Highest marks on his mid-term exams. Helped us push Mrs. Baxter's car out of the mud when it got stuck in the back field. And he didn't even *like* Mrs. Baxter.

"She got me suspended four times in grade eleven, and I wasn't even in her class! Still, bygones, right?"

April—no suspensions.

The first three weeks leading up to the prom in May—no suspensions.

And then he was sent to my office by Mr. Pringle. And Mr. Pringle sounded angry on the intercom.

"Forget's coming down to see you, and he'd better apologize!"

And then Mason was in my office, both confused and angry. "I have no idea why I'm here and no idea why I'm supposed to apologize! I gave him a friggin' compliment!"

"What's going on, Mason? What happened? And remember, you're not angry with me, right?"

"Yes, Sir. Sorry about the 'friggin.'"

"Now what happened?"

"Mr. Pringle's wearing a suit today. Something about a meeting after school or something. I've never seen him in a suit. He looks really good for an old guy. And so I told him that."

"You told him he looked good for an old guy?"

"Not in those words. I told him he looked like a pimp."

"A pimp? You told a sixty-year-old man he looked like a pimp?"

"Yeah! And he got all upset at me!"

"Mason, do you know what a pimp is?"

"Yeah! A guy who looks sharp!"

"Mason, you told a sixty-three-year-old man, who's wearing a suit to meet his daughter's fiancé for the first time, that he looks like a man who manages prostitutes. That's what a pimp is."

Mason's jaw dropped. "What? Well, that's not what I meant! How was I supposed to know that? I just thought that whenever they talk about the guys on TV wearing orange fur hats and things like that looking like pimps, I thought they meant those guys look sharp! I want one of those hats! Geez! I better go apologize! I like Pringle!"

And so Mason went back and delivered a heartfelt apology. He had no intention to insult and freely admitted his ignorance of what the word *really* meant, but to him, all it ever meant was someone who looked sharp. He would never call Mr. Pringle a pimp again. They shook hands and things were settled.

And then we got to the night of the prom. Unlike many schools, almost every teacher at Western Secondary School went to prom. It was a night of celebration for everyone. Teachers got there early and then watched the kids as they arrived. It was…interesting…what some kids thought they should wear to prom, but almost everyone looked sharp, from a forty-five-year-old principal's point of view. Mr. Eric Pringle and his wife were at my table that year. He'd decided that he was going to retire in June, and I asked if I could buy him and his wife tickets for that year's prom. And they'd agreed.

And then Mason Forget arrived. Our table went silent. I don't know if I can adequately describe his outfit. Purple pinstriped zoot suit. Black and white Oxford shoes.

Orange shirt. Purple tie. Two-foot, gold wallet chain. Orange fur hat.

He walked straight to our table. "Good evening Mr. Garlick. Mrs. Garlick. He shook our hands. Good evening Mr. Pringle. Mrs. Pringle. Congratulations on your upcoming retirement." He leaned forward and whispered something to Mr. Pringle, who started laughing as Mason Forget walked away.

"What did he say?" I asked.

Mr. Pringle wiped his eyes and calmed down after a few more seconds of laughing.

"He said, 'I look like a pimp, don't I?'"

Epilogue

Later that evening, as the students were leaving, Mason called me over to his car.

"I've got something to show you, Sir."

He popped the trunk to show me two cases of beer.

"Mason! Why are you showing me this!?"

"Nothing's opened, Sir. And nothing will be opened until my friends and I get back to my house and my mother has taken away all of their car keys. There are going to be twenty of us, so there's not enough here for any of us to get much of a buzz. And we're all legal. I mean of legal age. Like I told you, Sir. No more high school hijinks."

At graduation in June, when I shook Mason's hand, he was the only one that year who said, "A handshake's not enough, Sir." And then he gave me a bear hug and lifted me off my feet.

Two Embarrassing Situations

The Most Embarrassing Situation

I am breaking a promise by telling this story, but it's a promise I've already broken dozens of times, and it's a promise I made more to myself than anybody else. So I guess it's okay. I don't know whether the young woman who was part of the promise has broken it too, but if she has, that's also okay.

It makes for a really good story.

For years and years, Western Secondary School had a problem with wasps. I don't know whether it does now, but by the time I left the school, the problem was largely solved.

I was Death to wasps.

Every year, almost from the first day I was principal there, it was one of my goals to rid the school of the nasty little yellow-and-black stripey things. I'd seek out their nests and destroy them. In their dormancy, I'd knock the nests to the ground with a yard stick and stomp on them. When they were active, I'd spray them with wasp killer, then knock them to the ground with a yard stick and stomp on them.

In spite of killing literally thousands and thousands of wasps in this manner, I was only stung once, on my forehead, and not while I was knocking or spraying or stomping. I was sitting at my desk typing when one of the little bastards snuck in and stung me on the forehead.

A small price to pay for being Death to wasps.

Why did I have such a vendetta against the yellow-and-black stripey things?

It was the kids. A rather large number were deathly allergic to them and should have been carrying epinephrine auto-injectors, otherwise known as EpiPens, but they wouldn't. I had more than thirty of these EpiPens in the main office against the time a student would eat a peanut butter sandwich, or something with eggs, or encounter ragweed, or—most often—get stung by a wasp.

Teachers took the annual training on how to use an EpiPen very seriously, because although their use wasn't common, it wasn't exactly out of the ordinary either. Several of us could say with pride that we'd saved a kid's life with one of them.

And so, when Cindy Comstock (not her real name) came running into the main office crying, "I'VE BEEN

STUNG BY A WASP AND I'M GONNA DIE!" we all knew what to do. The attendance secretary went to the cabinet where we stored the EpiPens; the senior secretary called 911 and then Cindy's parents; and I ushered the young woman into my office and began the process of calming her down.

"You're not going to die, Cindy. Everything is going to be fine. Here. You can have a seat in my chair."

"I can? I've never been in the principal's office before. And I get to sit in *your* chair! Your desk is a bit of a mess, isn't it, Sir?"

She was already calming down.

"Well, I wasn't expecting guests!"

Cindy chuckled at this. She was still calming down. I was pretty good at this.

The attendance secretary brought me Cindy's EpiPen and left the office. She, like me, hated needles.

"Have you used one of these before, Cindy?"

"I CAN'T USE ONE OF THOSE THINGS! I'LL PASS OUT AND DROP IT!"

She was no longer calming down.

"Oh. Well that's not a problem. I've been trained. I know how to do it. Would it be okay if I used it on you?"

Sniffles... "I guess that'd be okay, but it's gonna hurt."

"Yes. It probably will, but only for ten seconds, and we can count together, okay?"

I knelt down in front of her. "I'm going to take the blue cap off this end, and hit your thigh with this end —okay? And then we'll count to ten together and it will all be over."

At this point, I need to tell you that Cindy Comstock (not her real name) was eighteen years old and one of the... most well-endowed young women in the school. The following events happened very quickly. Ten or eleven seconds to be exact.

I hit Cindy in the thigh. She grabbed my head by the ears and pulled it into her chest. I counted: "ONE—*pleasenobodycomeintomyoffice*—TWO—*pleasenobodycomeintomyoffice*—THREE—*pleasenobodycomeintomyoffice*—*" all the way to "TEN."

I pulled the needle from Cindy's thigh and she let go of my head.

I know why my face was red, but I wasn't sure if hers was red from embarrassment, or the almost immediate effect of the epinephrine.

"Oh, Mr. Garlick. I'm so sorry! I just wasn't expecting that to hurt as much as it did. Are you okay?"

"I'm fine, Cindy. But we don't tell *any*body about this, okay?"

"I promise, Sir."

"Me too."

(In case you're concerned. Cindy was fine. The ambulance came and took her to the hospital, which *has* to happen after a person's been given epinephrine. Her parents called to thank me and my staff for acting as quickly as we did and didn't mention the ten seconds of embarrassment, so I'm guessing Cindy didn't tell them straight away, anyway. Cindy was back at school the next day.

I kept my promise until the end of the school day, when I told my vice-principals, who laughed and laughed. And then when I got home I told my wife, who also laughed and laughed. I've told the story, as I mentioned at the beginning, dozens of times, whenever a small group talks about EpiPens or life-threatening allergies.

Or whenever I'm asked what my most embarrassing moment as principal was.

Another Embarrassing Situation

While I think that it's true that most students in Ontario dislike the provincial standardized tests, it's also true that almost all of them take these tests with minimal complaining.

They might complain at home, and they probably complain to each other, but they rarely complain to their teachers or principals. We're seen as allies. Kids know that there is almost anything we'd rather do than administer a test that's shipped to us from Toronto in large blue plastic boxes that have to be locked away in the school safe in the days leading up to the test.

Only one student complained in the fourth year of the test. Angela was new to our school and didn't understand that we were all on her side. On the day before the test, she announced to her class that she wasn't going to write it at all. "I wrote the stupid thing last year and I passed. I'm not taking it again."

"According to the records that your previous school sent us, that's not the case, and if you don't write it and pass, well, that means that next year you'll have to take the

Literacy Course, which is just the test spread out over a whole semester, and I can't imagine a more boring way to spend your last semester here."

"Nope. My last school is wrong. I passed and I'm not writing it again. I'm staying home to watch *Judge Judy*, or *Ellen*, or whoever is on TV in the morning. I don't care."

Well, as things turned out, the student lived in a group home and the leader of the group home was not about to have this student staying at home when she was supposed to be at school passing this test. So, although it sounds a bit over the top, the group home leader called the police who, for some reason, consented to pick the girl up and deliver her to our foyer just as the test was getting ready to start.

This caused Angela to lose her mind and she arrived in our foyer in a manner reminiscent of the Tasmanian Devil from the *Looney Tunes* cartoons of my youth. She was spinning angry when the police handed her off to us, saying, "Good Luck with her!" before leaving.

The girl was so loud that if I didn't do something quickly she was going to disrupt a large number of the kids who were about to write the test.

"Angela! ANGELA! Let's go into my office and we'll work this out!"

"THERE'S NOTHING TO WORK OUT! I'M NOT WRITING THE STUPID TEST AND YOU'RE GOING TO HAVE TO FIND SOME PLACE IN THIS BUILDING FOR ME TO YELL AND SCREAM FOR THE NEXT THREE HOURS. I MEAN IT!"

"You know what? I agree! Let's go call Toronto to let them know what we think about this!"

"What?"

"You're yelling at the wrong people. If you want to yell at the people responsible, you and I —*we*—should be yelling at someone in the Education Quality and Accountability Office, right?"

"I don't understand…" She was far calmer now, which confusion can do to a person.

"Let's go into my office and call the EQAO and find the correct person for you to complain to. I'll help." I started walking towards the office, turning to notice that Angela hadn't moved from the spot she'd been yelling at me from. "Are you coming?"

"You'd do that for me?"

"Sure! Come on!"

Writing this, in 2021, five years after I retired, I still remember the phone number for the EQAO, but only because I had to call it so many times over the years. One year they shipped us cartons of unlabeled cassette tapes that weren't going to be able to assist *any* of our visually impaired students. Another year, it was unlabeled CDs. In fact, almost every year from 2002 to 2016, I had to call the EQAO, so it's not really that impressive that I remember the 1-888 phone number.

I told Angela, "I've called the EQAO so often this spring that I don't even have to look the number up. Let's give them a call."

She sat down across from me at my desk and started to cry. She grabbed a tissue from the box on my desk and wiped her eyes. "I don't really want to yell at anybody Mr. Garlick… I can't believe how nice you're being to me… Let's not yell at them, okay? They just made a mistake, that's all…"

I said, "Okay. Tell you what. Let's call the EQAO and see if they can help you. If they say you don't have to write, I'll call you a cab and you can go back home, okay?"

And with that, I picked up the phone, saying, once again, that I'd called the number *very* often and dialed, but I didn't dial 1-888, to be honest, I don't know *what* number I dialed, but a very sultry and breathy voice on the other end of the phone said,

"Hey Big Boy, I'm really glad you called!"

I hung up immediately, slamming the phone into its cradle, looking shocked, and Angela started laughing. "How often did you say you called that number, Sir?"

And then we were both laughing. Me, a bit more red in the face than she was.

In the end, it turned out that Angela was correct. She *had* passed the test the year before. I picked up the phone to call her a cab—another phone number I had memorized.

"Tell you what, Sir. I don't need to go home. I'll go ask Chef if he needs any help today. Maybe he'll let me help make lunch for the rest of the kids."

And when she got to my office door, she turned and said, "Sir? Thanks for everything today… and I've never thought of you as a Big Boy."

She left the office laughing.

Shukri's Short Story

Throughout my career, I was fortunate to work with excellent, excellent, student leaders, particularly our student prime ministers. I refuse to rank them, because they were *all* wonderful, all exceptional. However, none was more exceptional than Shukri Abdulle, who was the student prime minister of Forster Secondary School for its final two years.

She was elected prime minster when she was in grade ten.

Think of that.

In grade ten, you're fourteen years old; at that age, she threw her hat in the ring and was *elected* prime minister in a school of more than 700 kids.

Exceptional.

And then she ran again, and won again, when she was in grade eleven.

She was a joy. Hard working, pleasant, always in a good mood, killer smile, and bright, bright, bright. And she was respected by every student and staff member.

(Now that I think of it, this describes just about every prime minister I worked with over the years.)

Anyway, it was 2013. I forget what the issue was, but teachers were upset with the provincial government. As principal, I was not allowed to officially take sides, but I'd been teaching for thirty years by this point, and almost always, in my opinion, the teachers were justified when they were upset. This time was no different.

Instead of going on strike and walking off the job, which only *really* happened once in my career, teachers had decided to "work to rule," holding informational pickets at lunch. Whatever the issue was, the students of the school also supported the teachers, so at the beginning of lunch, everybody emptied out of the building, like a fun sort of fire alarm, except there was no alarm and everybody had gone onto the front lawn.

Throughout the province, there was talk of kids not returning to class when the bell rang, but the kids told me that they'd head back in after lunch. There'd also been talk that kids had been *brainwashed* by the teachers and didn't understand the issues at all. And while it may be true that some of the kids didn't understand the issues, I think that that just proves that the teachers *hadn't* been brainwashing the kids. If they had, the kids would at least all know one side, right?

I went out front along with everyone else to make sure that everyone stayed safe, not going onto the road and stopping traffic.

I walked up to the first senior I saw and I said, "Okay. So let's say that a reporter from the *Windsor Star*, or the CBC or CKLW, shows up. They stop you and say, 'What's going on? Why is everyone out here?' What do you say to them?"

"Well, Sir…I'd say… It's kinda like World War Two…"

"So now the reporter looks a bit confused, because that's certainly not the answer he was expecting. But he asks you to explain…"

"Well Sir? It's like the provincial government are the Germans… and the teachers… are the Jews!"

I hadn't seen Shukri walk up behind us as we were talking. She smiled as she touched his elbow and said, "So if a reporter from the *Windsor Star*, or the CBC or CKLW, shows up… You don't talk to *anybody*, okay?"

"Yeah… That's probably best," said the senior, to the girl in grade ten.

A Christmas Memory

I don't want to get into ranking these things. The fact is that after almost thirty-five Christmases in education, I have many Christmas memories, and I don't wish to rank them. Each of them is my favourite. This is one of them.

There's no need for me to change names or fictionalize this story at all. This is exactly how I remember it:

Let me start by stating that Forster Secondary School was our Board's English as a Second Language School. More than seventy different countries were represented by the students at this school. And every year, teachers expressed the concern that maybe we shouldn't be celebrating Christmas, because we didn't want to offend the non-Christians. This was at the same time that letters to the editor appeared in the paper complaining about the "War on Christmas," as though there was a concerted effort by nefarious elements of society to end the holiday. But every year, it was the students of all faiths who almost demanded that we observe the holiday.

"Where do we put the tree, Mr. Garlick? Do we all get to decorate it?"

"Are we going to have a door decorating contest again this year? It was so much fun last year, although my class should have won!"

"Is it true that the staff makes breakfast for us on the last day before break?"

"I hope we have an ugly sweater contest again this year. Mr. Yaworsky's was great last year!"

We tried to recognize *all* the major holidays throughout the year, so they thought it only fair that Christmas was celebrated as well, and it was the students of these other faiths who took the lead in organizing the Christmas parties for the feeder schools.

When I was principal of Forster Secondary School, every year we held a Christmas party for the kindergarten students from our feeder schools. We'd make each student a gift bag with a book, a colouring book and crayons, and some treats, all of which was given to them by Santa Claus. I don't really remember what all else we did, because I was asked to be Santa Claus each year. I'm pretty sure we gave the children a lunch: a hot dog and potato chips, and a juice. We almost certainly sang songs, and our band would have performed for them. But I don't really *know* all this, because I wasn't there for that part of things.

I was the main event. *I* was Santa Claus.

So, as the party was starting, I was always in my office trying to figure out how to put on the Santa suit, stuff the jacket with a pillow, put the beard and moustache on over my head and figure out if I could still wear my glasses while wearing it. (You forget all these things from year to year.)

This never took very long, but I had to greet the students as they arrived—as the principal, not as Santa—because I wanted the kids to be able to go home and tell their parents they met the Principal *and* Santa Claus. So I was a bit rushed.

I then had to practise my baritone, "Ho, ho, ho," because it's not something you do throughout the year, and you don't want it to sound forced or fake. It's not as easy as you might think.

So I was in my office, dressed as Santa, practising my "Ho, ho, ho," when I heard someone else, outside my office also saying "Ho, ho, ho."

I didn't *think* someone was mocking Santa, but to be honest, I had no idea why somebody else would be saying, "Ho, ho, ho." I'd been assured that I was going to be the Santa of the day; that there weren't going to be competing Santas at school that day, just to confuse the four and five year olds.

I walked into the main office from my office and saw through the glass wall to the hallway that there was, indeed, another Santa in the main hall, with a large red sack. The kindergarteners were all in the auditorium by this point, so this Santa was only passing out candy canes to Forster students and Forster teachers that were passing by him in the hall. There was no confusion for the four- and five-year-olds because they were all listening to the Forster band, or eating hot dogs or cookies or whatever.

"Confronting" is the wrong word for what I did, because there was only curiosity behind my walking into the hall to see this other Santa. So when we saw each other we both began laughing genuine laughs. Not ho, ho, hos, but genuine laughs.

This other Santa turned out to be a parent of two of my favourite students that year. Two of my favourite *new Canadian* students. Two of my favourite *Muslim new Canadian* students. And this parent was their *mother*.

After we'd finished laughing, she smiled, reached deep into her sack and pulled out a wrapped little box and presented it to me.

"Merry Christmas, Mr. Garlick."

Doing the Right Thing

There was a teacher at one of my schools whose real name I won't mention here. Karen was definitely not her real name. She was a fine teacher. The kids loved her. There was never a complaint about her from any student or any parent or teacher. But every once in a while, she created work for me.

"Dave, you really need to be on Facebook. You have no idea what these kids get up to on the weekends!"

"And I don't want to know! Karen, technically, I'm allowed to suspend any kid for anything they do, no matter when they do it, if it makes its way into the school and negatively affects the school environment. But if I suspend one kid for one thing you tell me about, I've got to suspend every kid for every thing I hear about! So don't tell me!"

This teacher was a widow, living on her own, and I'm sure she spent evenings, with a yearbook in her hands, "creeping" the kids on Facebook. That's what it's called when you navigate through social media looking at other people's sites, at the information they're foolish enough to put out there for their "friends," not realizing anyone, even well-meaning, middle-aged widows, can see.

"You know Dave. They're selling drugs across the street right under your nose!" She said to me one Wednesday afternoon.

"Across the street isn't under my nose," I answered.

"You know what I mean. They're selling drugs and you're not doing anything about it!"

"I'm out there every day at lunch! They are not selling drugs across the street."

"You can be so naive! They wait until you leave! And you do nothing about it!"

"If they wait until I leave, how can I so something about it? You've just said I'm not there!"

She paused, momentarily stymied by my logic. "Well, you could hide in the bushes…"

"No. *We* can hide in the bushes! Or better yet, we can hide in McMurtry's house at lunch!"

"What?"

"*I* don't think the kids are selling drugs across the street. Oh, I know that some of them *use* drugs, but *I* don't think they're stupid enough to sell them right out front of the school. *You* think they are. So, this Friday, which is the day they would be buying and selling drugs for the weekend, you and I will be in Mr. McMurtry's living room across the street. He'll be happy to help and we'll watch the kids. If we see anyone buying or selling drugs I'll suspend them, okay?"

So that's what we did. We ate lunch with Mr. McMurtry, a school neighbour, bringing him a pizza, and watched the kids for forty minutes and saw... nothing. Well, nothing untoward. No drug sales. No drug use. Nothing.

"Still, you should really be on Facebook. You'd see what they get up to."

"They get up to enough right here. We've got as much work as we need. I don't need to go looking for more, and neither do you."

And then, a month later, while I was still at school, but it was getting late, I received a short text from Karen. "Sending picture through now!"

And then a picture came through of one of my students, smiling for the camera. By himself. Full camouflage and grease paint, in his bathroom I guess, holding what looked like an assault rifle.

Not really breaking any laws. Might not even be a real gun. Still...

I had to do something. The very least that would happen if I did nothing was that a story would quickly spread through the staff room, then the union, that I'd been sent a picture of a kid with an assault rifle and I'd done nothing.

I didn't even want to think about the worst that could happen.

I texted Karen back immediately. "I'm calling the police now. Say nothing about this until I get back to you."

And then I called the police. "Sir, it may take up to an hour for an officer to respond. Can you wait for the officers at school?"

"Ma'am, no. I've already been here for twelve hours. I'm tired and I'm hungry. Would it be all right if I printed off all the information I have on this student, address, phone number, that kind of thing, and talk to the officers at my house?"

So then I called Karen back, told her what I'd done, and told her I'd speak to her in the morning when we knew more. "This may be nothing at all. So please, don't talk to anyone about it right now. There's no need to worry anyone else."

"Are *you* worried, Dave?"

"A bit, yes."

"Good. Me too."

So I drove home, had dinner with my wife, and told her why the police would be stopping by shortly. But they didn't. They didn't arrive until after eight-thirty.

The officers that did arrive were two officers in full SWAT gear. I'm sure the neighbours talked about that!

"Sorry, Sir. We had a man barricaded in his home and concern about possible explosives. We came straight here after that was resolved. Peacefully, by the way. No explosives."

I explained why I called and what I knew about the student. I gave them a copy of the picture the teacher had sent me. "Listen, he's a really good kid. When you talk with him, can you call me and let me know what happened? I've got at least one teacher to talk to about this."

"Yes Sir. But be sure to thank her. No matter what happens, it was a really smart idea to call. You can't be too careful these days."

They came back about an hour later. And again, I'm sure the neighbours talked.

"It turns out that the picture was quite old, from before he even came to Canada. He'd been in the military in his home country before coming here. Proud of his service. He showed us some other pictures too. Vouched for by his parents and his older sister. He understood your concern, though, and he's taken the picture down."

I called the teacher before going to bed. I told her about everything that had happened and how the picture was completely innocent. I also told her that under no circumstances was she to talk about this with any of the staff. "Just leave the kid alone, okay?"

"Yes, Dave."

"But Karen? Thanks for looking out for the school and for trusting me to do the right thing."

I Hate High School Swimming Pools

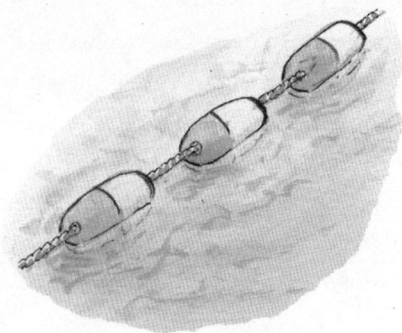

I hate high school swimming pools. Well, that's not entirely accurate. I don't hate *all* high school swimming pools. Just one, really. I hate the swimming pool at J. L. Forster Secondary School. And to be fair, that one is closed, along with the school, which I do *not* hate.

I don't hate the pool because I had to swim naked in it in grade nine; and yes, that was an entirely normal thing in the late '60s and early '70s, and no, my teacher wasn't a pervert—every boys' gym class in Ontario had to swim naked in the '60s and early '70s. The Ministry of Health decided that was preferable to boys leaving their swimming trunks in their lockers for weeks and then swimming in those same trunks. The Ministry was probably right. Boys couldn't be trusted with basic hygiene. And I don't hate that swimming pool because it was over-chlorinated and made my eyes burn, although it was and it did. My hatred for the pool didn't really develop until I was a principal.

I always had great Phys. Ed. teachers at Forster. And the boys' Phys. Ed. teacher was a particularly good swimming instructor, Dylan Lanspeary. Top notch. Finest kind. Dylan was maybe even more concerned with pool safety than I was. He ensured that multiple students in each class were qualified in CPR and artificial respiration. And it didn't make a difference what grade he was teaching, every swimming unit started with the procedures to follow in case of an "incident."

My hatred for the pool was because all this training became necessary. Every year.

Every year, some kid would swim at full speed into the wall of the swimming pool and knock himself out, sinking quickly to the bottom. Dylan would dive into the pool to rescue him as another student ran to the emergency phone to call an ambulance and another would run to the front of the school to wait and guide the ambulance attendants and another student would run to the main office to inform me so I could call the parents to let them know what had just happened. And every year Dylan saved the kid's life and I would commend him and his class.

Every year.

One year, two kids swam into each other, knocking themselves out, so Dylan had to rescue two kids at once and two ambulances had to come to the school and I had to call two sets of parents.

No one ever died.

But, man! Every year!

I was secretly very happy when the Board announced that they were going to shut the pool down. This was before they'd decided to close the school. The pool was more than seventy years old, and apparently would have cost more than a quarter million dollars to repair. I had to take the Board's word for this. The pool itself looked pretty good for something I hated so much. But the "guts" of the pool, the pump and the over-chlorinator, were another matter. They were located underneath the pool itself and were accessed through our cafeteria, which was in the basement of the school, but that's another story. This room under the pool looked far more ancient than the pool itself. The under-room looked like something from an Edgar Allan Poe short story, always looking and feeling dank and dreary, as though maybe some former student who hadn't been rescued in some previous year had been walled up down there.

Still, I thought that maybe the Board was pulling my chain, and that the true cost of repair was closer to $700. I mean, what had changed? The pool had been the pool for seventy years! What could be so bad?

I privately believed that, although I never spoke to anyone about it, but I was happy to go along with the story that the repairs would cost a quarter million dollars. I believed it until I happened to see two maintenance workers emerge from the under-room. They both looked like they'd seen a ghost, and although I thought the under-room *looked* like it belonged in a story by Mr. Poe, I doubted that they'd actually seen a ghost.

"The pool's being de-commissioned this summer, right?" they asked me.

"Yup. In August."

They looked back at the now closed door. "It might hold until then."

"What does that mean?"

"Well... If it doesn't hold... All the water in *there* will end up *here*," they said, indicating the cafeteria.

I hated that pool.

Tuberculosis and the Health Unit

Because of COVID-19 and the reality of 2020–2021, most people now have a passing knowledge of the Ministry of Health and their local health unit. I gained my initial, first-hand experience of the Health Unit because of a very different issue: tuberculosis.

To be honest, I didn't know much about the condition. I knew that it used to be known as consumption and that King John of England had died from it, as had Doc Holiday who became famous at the Gunfight at the O.K. Corral. And that Dickensian sufferers coughed quietly into white linen handkerchiefs and took cures by journeying to Egypt. North American sufferers went to Arizona.

But that was about it, really. Oh, I also knew about our city's sanitarium and that I had two aunts who had acquired TB in the 1940s or early '50s. I knew that it wasn't a death sentence anymore and was treatable with antibiotics, but again, not much more than that.

And then I sent a student to the hospital after he collapsed and threw up blood in the office.

I spent a large part of that evening on my computer researching TB. Did you know, for instance, that almost a quarter of the people on the planet are currently estimated to be infected? And that the vast majority of those people will never know it, and have no symptoms, and will probably never have symptoms? And those people can't give it to anyone? The only people who can transmit TB are the unlucky few who are infected, and then the virus, for them, becomes active, usually because their immune system is compromised through another illness. Those people can transmit it really easily, by coughing, spitting, or even just breathing on you.

I received a phone call from the health unit the next day asking if they could come talk with me. The student had tested positive for TB. and was in isolation at the hospital. They told me that they were beginning contact tracing, a term I'd never heard, but they explained: "Think of it as a series of expanding circles. We start by testing his immediate family. If any of them test positive, we make the circle bigger, and test them. Say his friends or neighbours in his apartment building if he lives in an apartment building. If any of them test positive, we'll come to your school and test his classmates, and anyone who's come into contact with him here."

"So you'll be testing the whole school…"

"I didn't say that. Just the kids he's come in contact with."

"It'll be the school… My kids come from over seventy different countries. What are the chances that *none* of his classmates will test positive? I've been here for seven years, and at Lowe for six years before that. Honestly, I'd be surprised to find out I'm not infected."

"Mr. Garlick, I think you're over-stating the case."

"We'll see. I hope you're right, but I think I am." And in the end, I was right.

Before that turned out to be the case, I called the Board to let them know. They told me to do whatever the health unit told me to do, which is exactly what I'd planned on. I called an urgent staff meeting after school, had one of the health unit nurses assist me, and broke things as matter-of-factly and calmly as I could. The staff took it pretty well, I thought.

I quickly arranged for a series of small assemblies to be held as soon as we knew they'd be testing the school, and I arranged for a group of translators to be at the school for my English language learners.

The health unit let the media know, doing their best to be factual and informative with them. This was, at present, a single student, and he was responding to treatment and improving.

The media were having none of that. It wasn't nearly exciting enough. They interviewed my superintendent, who did a great job in my opinion, with the interviewer doing his best to find a scandal that didn't exist. He was clearly frustrated with the superintendent's matter of fact attitude, her actual knowledge, and the fact that she wasn't pulling out her hair and screaming. When he finished interviewing her, he turned to the camera and said, and I quote: "If you want to know more about this situation, I recommend you call your trustee or anyone else."

"Or anyone else?" What would that even mean?

One thing it meant was that they called me. Which wasn't bad. Most of the people who called were parents just looking to be reassured their son or daughter wasn't dying. They were calm and looking for answers. I set up assemblies for them as well.

Only one parent started out unreasonable, in my opinion. "Listen Mr. Garlick! I want you to walk my son out to the car right now! And he won't be coming back until every kid in your f-ing school is checked out and cleared, okay? And when you come out you'd better be wearing a f-ing mask!"

"Sir? If you do that right now, how will you know if your son isn't infected?"

"What?"

"If you want us all tested and checked out to make sure *we* don't have it, how will you know your son isn't infected if he's not tested? If the health unit tells me to have the school tested, we'll be tested, but shouldn't that include your son?"

Silence.

"Okay… I'll take him out to lunch today. And bring him back after that, okay?"

"Sure. And if the health unit says to test him, we can get him tested, right? We have to get your permission."

"Oh… Okay. Say, do you think they'd test me? I mean, I'm around my kid a lot!"

As I said, it turned out that I was right, and that the whole school would have to be tested, which involved more work than you can imagine. Letters of permission, written and translated into a dozen languages; special schedules; far more than just setting up the auditorium with, I forget, ten stations, twelve maybe? A sitting area for kids to wait for ten minutes after their test, in case they fainted. Mats to lay them on should they faint. At the stations, kids would be asked a series of questions and then given the TB test, which is just a needle under a couple layers of skin on the inside of the forearm, and then injected with a small amount of something that creates a small bubble, like a small blister. Painless, even for someone like me. And yet, kids still fainted. Not a huge number—three or four, five maybe, but enough to cause worry in the kids who were lined up waiting.

And then two days later, the health unit was back to "read" the tests. If that small blister had gotten bigger, I think with a diameter of larger than a centimeter, and angry red, you were advised to go get a chest x-ray to confirm that you weren't active, and you were also advised to take a series of pretty strong antibiotics which give you a ninety percent chance of never becoming active.

So how many kids were infected? I've no idea. If the kids didn't want to tell me, they didn't have to. Remember, if they aren't active, they have no way of giving it to me, and if they were active, they'd be hospitalized. How many teachers were infected? Again, I have no way of knowing. I think many thought there would be a stigma with being positive, and so they wouldn't talk about it—but the reality, again, was they could have been infected for years. They could have been infected at the mall, or while grocery shopping, or while vacationing in Mexico or Tahiti or anywhere.

I know I wasn't infected. And I was surprised to find that out.

Later on the day of the test readings, I heard from the health unit again. This time, it had nothing to do with TB or anyone else in my school.

At lunch, I was out front of the school talking with the kids, as I tried to do every day. "No, I'm not infected. You?" "Were you scared?" "What do your parents think about all this?" Those were the conversation starters of the day.

And then I saw a man walking his dog. My school had a large number of Muslim students who had a natural... disdain is too strong a word. Aversion is closer. Fear is pretty good—a fear of dogs. Whenever I had the chance, I tried to show the kids that dogs were actually pretty cool. My wife brought our dog, Mitzy the Wonderdog, to school every once in a while. Mitzy was a great ambassador for Dogdom.

So anyway, I walked up to the man and his dog and said, "That's a fine looking dog, Sir! May I pet her?"

"Sure! This is Misha! She loves being petted!"

And indeed, the dog's tail was wagging. "Please Sir! Pet me!" she said, in Dog.

So I reached down, showing the dog my empty hand, and she reached forward and bit me. Took half my hand in her mouth and chomped down. Just the once.

I pulled my hand back, looking at my palm. No damage done.

"Gee! She's never done that before! You okay?"

"I think so…" but then I turned my hand over. Blood was streaming from the scrapes of Misha's bottom teeth. "I guess not…"

"Sorry! Like I said, she's never done anything like this before. But she has been acting kind of strange lately…"

Great, I thought. "Has she had her shots?"

"I don't know. I've only had her for a couple months. I guess I'll have to call the previous owner, eh?"

And so we exchanged information. Name, address, phone number. And I went to my doctor for a tetanus shot. I was due anyway.

Later that evening, I received another phone call from the health unit. From a nurse who'd never heard of me, one I hadn't been talking to for the last two weeks.

"We're calling just to let you know that the owner of a dog named Misha called us about you, and that we have the dog under quarantine. If she develops rabies or distemper in that time, we'll call you. If not, there aren't any concerns. Do you have any questions for me?"

Loneliness in G Minor

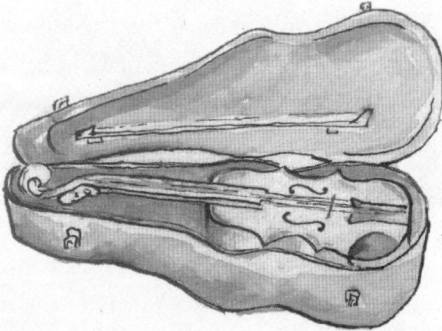

I came back to school one evening in October after supper. I forget why. It was dark outside, so it was, what, 7:30 p.m.? 8:00? Maybe even a bit later.

As I entered the back door by the parking lot, the lights came on in the hall. I still wasn't used to the motion-detecting lights which came on as you'd enter and walk down a hallway. Both money-saving and a bit unnerving.

As I got closer to the front of the school, I heard the most beautiful music. A single violin. Plaintive and a bit heart-breaking, but beautiful. I stopped to listen before rounding the corner and turning the lights on. I noticed that the lights in the hallway where the music was coming from were off as well, which meant that whoever was

creating that lovely music was not moving enough to acti-
vate them, and hadn't been for long enough that they had
switched off and stayed off. Playing alone in the dark. I
hoped the music would go on and on, but it stopped after
another minute, and then the lights came on. I turned
the corner.

A young girl was sitting in the foyer, packing up her
violin. I recognized her from talking with her just the previous week. She was in grade nine and she'd been sitting
by herself at lunch. A lot of kids did that, sat in the hall at
lunch by themselves, and I usually stopped to say "Hi" to
them and introduce myself. Her name, if I remembered
correctly, was Casey, which she preferred to Cassandra.

She looked up and saw me. "Mr. Garlick! I'm so sorry!
I'll go home right now! I shouldn't have stayed so long.
I'm sorry!"

"No, no. It's okay, Casey, it's fine. That was beautiful! I
hope you don't mind; I listened to most of it from around
the corner."

She smiled when I mentioned her name, pleased
that I'd remembered it. "Thank you... So... I'm not in
any trouble?"

"Not with me, no. But do your parents know where
you are? It's getting kind of late."

"They think I'm at the house of a friend who lives
around the corner from here. I don't like to lie, but I find
that the acoustics are perfect here in the foyer, and I don't
ever get to play here without people around. The custodians are all upstairs by now, so I'm not bothering them,
either. I *do* know someone who lives around here, so

getting home won't be any more dangerous than it would be if I was there."

"Well, maybe you should be getting home anyway. It is kind of late to be out on a school night."

"Yes, Sir."

"That piece *was* beautiful though. What's it called?"

"It's called 'Loneliness in G Minor.'"

"Well, it's beautiful. Have a nice night, Casey."

"You too, Mr. Garlick."

I walked the little remaining distance to the main office as Casey finished packing up. Just as I was putting my key in the office door, she said,

"Mr. Garlick?"

"Yes?"

"I wrote it. Tonight."

Haircuts and Barbershops and Baldness and Beards

In 1992, I gained a little bit of local notoriety because of the beard I grew for the city's Centennial Beard-Growing Contest. On the first of January, all entrants had to present themselves, clean-shaven, at the city's Centennial Office. And then, on the first of July, all those same people assembled at the Riverfront Plaza for the judging ceremony. I had a secret weapon in Roger, who was my former student and current hair stylist.

To be honest, *style* and my hair have never gone together very well. The "Regular Boy's Haircut" of the

1960s had made way for the Number 2 blend, but that was about it for my head. However, my beard was another matter. Roger knew of the competition and was eager to help, so when I went to him in March and said, "Roger, make me look like Czar Nicholas," he was all set. I just had to tell him who Czar Nicholas was and show him some pictures of Russian royalty.

Throughout March, April, May, and June, Roger worked on my beard, and from January to July, my beard did everything it could to help. The reality is that everyone's hair grows at pretty much the same rate, so nobody's beard could have been that much longer than anyone else's, but mine had months of attention from a master.

The only "spanner in the works" for me was that I needed surgery on my face in March, and for a couple weeks it looked as though I would have to withdraw from the competition. It was odd that this was my biggest concern, given that there was a fair-to-good chance that the lumps the surgeon had to remove were cancerous, but that's how it was. When I finally had my consult with the surgeon, he took a marker and drew on my face and neck where his incision would go. "If you don't mind a goatee for a few weeks, you can keep most of your beard," he told me. I was as elated to hear this as I was after the surgery to hear that the tumours weren't cancerous. To look like Czar Nicholas, a bushy beard wasn't needed. Long and trimmed to a point, with a really jazz moustache, was the thing.

I was not really surprised, therefore, when I won the contest on the first of July. The prize was a thousand dollars and my picture on the front page of the paper.

Now, for someone who's spent years with a Number 2 blend and a beard, you might think that this would be the most fame I could earn with my head and face. Not so. I became relatively famous in the local education business as an administrator, not because of anything even vaguely educational, but because of my beard—well, half of it.

I don't know why it was such a big deal, but on pretty much an annual basis, I'd bet the kids that if they'd bring in so many cans in the annual Christmas can drive, I'd shave off my beard. If they raised even more than what I'd challenged them, I'd shave off *half* of my beard. More still, and I'd dye the remaining half a school colour.

And I'd leave it like that for a *week*!

The kids thought this was *crazy*! Someone would always call the local newspaper, and even though I did this, as I said, on a pretty much annual basis, the newspaper reporters would always show up, take a bunch of pictures, and run the story on page two. You can look it up.

The kids thought that this must be incredibly embarrassing for me, because I'd go to the mall, the grocery store, principal meetings, and everywhere I'd normally go, with my blue or red or yellow half-beard. And every year, I'd remind them of my secret. First off, *I* was the one who made the bet. Every year. If it was really that embarrassing, I probably wouldn't do it every year. Secondly, no matter where I went, people would always stop me and ask me why I had a blue or a red or a yellow half-beard (they clearly hadn't read the paper that week), and I got to tell them what great kids I had at my school.

But every year, it seemed, the kids all forgot, and then the newspaper would forget, and I'd have my half-beard face in the news again. "Garlick's *crazy*!"

And every year, there would be at least one kid who'd say, "Don't shave off your beard... Shave your *head*!" as though that was somehow a much bigger deal.

"Timmy," I'd say, or "Joanie," or "Sarkis, if I shave my head and go to the mall, all that will happen will be that a lot of people will say to themselves, 'Look at that poor, ugly man with that ugly, bald head.' I do not have a head for baldness."

Plus—and I rarely mentioned this—I *knew* that if I were to shave my head there was a very good chance that my hair would not grow back. That was my fear, anyway. My father is pretty much bald, and has been for a very long time. From a very early age, one of my many fears was that I, too, would go bald.

My reason for thinking this, apart from my father? I couldn't—and still can't—think of almost any male older than I am who is blond. Well, except for my brother, but he doesn't count. He's related to me, and not that much older. I know what many of you are thinking right now: Robert Redford. *Because he's the only one!*

Now there are probably a lot more. But go ahead—name three.

So, from the time I saw *Butch Cassidy and the Sundance Kid* in 1969, he was my favourite actor. Still is one of my top five or six, fifty-plus years later.

Anyway, this isn't about Robert Redford, or even my beard, really. This is about the fact—and I don't know how normal this was—that there was a barber shop less than a block from my house when I was a very young boy, less than seven years old. This was Adolfo's. And there was a barber *school* less than two blocks away. Haircuts at the barber school were only fifty cents. But even though they were really very inexpensive, I only remember going there the once.

I remember this, even though I was four years old, only because my mother screamed when my father brought me in the door. I'd never heard her scream before, nor have I heard her scream since. So, yes, memorable. If there had been cell phones then, my father would probably have called my mother to warn her not to scream. But there weren't, so he didn't, so she did.

My father told my mother they gave me the "cut" for free, because he was so angry.

I guess it was one of those situations where the left side was just a little longer than the right side, so the student had to shorten the left side, which was then a little shorter than the right side, and so on until—without asking anybody—the student just shaved my head. My father had been reading a magazine.

As I said earlier, I do not have the head for the Michael Jordan look. And apparently, I didn't have it when I was four years old, either.

So, from then on, it was Adolfo's for me. Seventy-five cents, well worth the extra money for no screaming when I got home. From the age of five (it took a year for my hair to grow back to the point where I needed to have it cut), my mother trusted me with seventy-five cents and the walk by myself to the corner. I don't know why my brother didn't get his hair cut at the same time, but I was allowed to go alone.

Before each cut, my mother would coach me. "And what are you going to ask for?"

"A regular boy's haircut."

"Yes. You are *not* to ask for a buzz cut. You are *not* to ask for him to shave your head. Okay?"

I have no idea why she was worried I would ask for a buzz cut. I mean, my brother often had a buzz cut, and he *was* my big brother, but this was 1965 and the Beatles were big. I had no desire to look like a throwback to the '50s. Even the regular boy's haircut was too short for me.

From 1965 to 1967, I'd walk up the street to Adolfo's, sit down to wait, and then get my haircut. The stand out memory of all this, in addition to the smell of the barber-shop, which I loved and still love, and the lemon tree in the window, was that as soon as I sat down to wait, Adolfo would say, "You can look at those magazines there, but not *those* magazines *there*. You look at *those* magazines, I shave you bald, okay?" As he cut my hair, he would always ask me if I wanted sideburns, which I wouldn't be able to actually grow until I was sixteen or seventeen.

In 1967, we moved about four blocks away to a new house. I wasn't sure if Mom would let me walk *four* blocks by myself, but I never got the chance to find out, because Adolfo moved to a new store, again less than a block from my home! I don't think he was following us, and he remained at that location for the rest of his career—in fact, until he died—and every once in a while I'd go back to him, right up until I was in my fifties.

For a short time, in my teens, I went to the Golden Razor, in the mall. A fancy place. Attractive young women would *wash* my hair before cutting it, but it cost considerably more than seventy-five cents. I decided that places like the Golden Razor were nice, but weren't really for me, the Number 2 blend guy. So I returned to Adolfo.

As a teacher, and then as a principal, my schools were always a short walk from a barber shop. I don't know if this is common either. I liked Vito, of Vito's, who always gave me a good haircut in ten minutes and would often say, "You a hairy guy. Whatsa matter with you?" As someone who still worried about going bald, this was somewhat comforting, but I think he was actually referring to my ears, eyebrows and nose, though I never asked.

Giuliano, of Giuliano's, always complained about something. Always. Never about me, but always about something. Sometimes it was the mayor and city council. Sometimes it was taxes. Sometimes it was the people who ticketed his customers if they forgot to feed the parking meter. "Bastards!" he'd yell. I worried about a man who was so upset being so close to my head and neck with scissors and razors, so I stopped going to him.

Johnny, of Johnny's, was very mild mannered and a really good barber, but the clientele were… suspect?… no, that's not the right word… weird. That's better. The middle-aged man sitting next to me might say, for example, out of nowhere, "Those people, they piss you off, don't they?" And I'd say, "What people?" And he'd say, "Oh they *don't*, eh? Johnny, I'll come back when you're finished with *this* guy, okay? He bugs me!" Someone else would just open the door to say, "No time this month. See you in September." And it would *be* September. I got to worrying that if all the other customers were a bit weird, maybe I was too. Plus, I didn't like sitting in the barber's chair when Mr. ThosePeoplePissYouOff walked by, as he seemed to whenever I was in the chair. He'd just stare, eyes glued on mine, as he walked past the shop, not watching where he was walking until he passed by.

When I was at Western Secondary School, we weren't *near* anything. In the middle of corn fields and, literally, miles to the closest town. But Western was a vocational school, so *kids* cut my hair. And they were happy with ten bucks! Which, by the early 2000s, was the equivalent, I guess, of fifty cents. And they never messed up! Barber schools had improved.

The only place cheaper than this was a mostly women's hair salon I'd pass on the way home from school. One day I noticed an advertisement painted in the window, with the same type of paint used at Christmas to paint winter scenes of trees and hills and Santa. "MEN'S haircuts: $8!" I couldn't resist. I was the only man in the place; the only customer without blue-tinted hair, to be honest. The woman who cut my hair pretended that it was entirely a normal thing to be cutting a man's hair; pretended, too, to understand what I meant when I asked for my standard Number 2 blend. She sat me down, took off my glasses, turned on the clippers, and said, five seconds later, "Ohthatsshort!" All one word.

She'd forgotten to put the Number 2 attachment on the clippers, and had just trimmed the side of my head almost bald. She did her best to leave me with some hair on the top of my head, and while my wife didn't scream when I got home, she echoed what the stylist had said, "Oh! That's short!"

It took about six months until I needed a haircut again. And I haven't been back. I *did* notice that the "MEN'S haircuts" painting was removed shortly after that. I guess I was part of a failed experiment.

When I retired, I started going to Carmine, of Carmine's, who gives children haircuts for free if they read him a story. I like that, and like him. I also went to Gentlemen's Choice, which is run by a former student, and they give customers free coffee or espresso or hot chocolate while they wait. I like that too, and I like him.

But then COVID hit, and I couldn't go to *anybody*. So after waiting until I looked like Ludwig von Beethoven, my wife said, "Do you want me to try to cut your hair?" And you know what? She does an excellent job! And I can get a coffee if I want. And I am either the weirdest or least weird customer in the place. And she doesn't complain. So I think I'll keep going to her.

But there's no lemon tree. And now that I'm old enough to look at them, I guess, I don't really need to look at *those* magazines.

The Keys to Being a Good Neighbour

There are two things you should know before I tell you this story: first, I live in a "nice neighbourhood." The kind of neighbourhood where we look out for each other. The kind where, if your next door neighbour goes away for a vacation, you'll take in their mail and water their plants, maybe even cut their lawn for them. The kind where you know most people by their first or last names, and new people on the block are both welcomed with a loaf of banana bread and viewed with suspicion for a few years. A nice neighbourhood.

The second thing you should know is that my next door neighbour, Ken, is a "car guy." He is an executive for Chrysler, and he loves cars. He collects them the way other people collect stamps. He knows what makes them work and fixes them in his driveway on his off days. He ensures though, that his wife, Deb, and all their children have Chrysler vehicles. That makes for a lot of cars when the family gets together for birthday parties and such. Now though, only son Kyle and daughter Paige are living there. Oh. I guess that a third thing you should know is that I am decidedly *not* a car guy. The one I own gets me places I need to get to and I know how to put in gasoline and when I should get an oil change.

Anyway, last Friday, my good friend Don Wilson retired from work after forty-three years as a city planner. My wife and I attended his retirement party, four blocks from our nice neighbourhood, in his nice neighbourhood. It was a wonderful affair. Lots of food, good conversation, champagne and anything else you would want to drink. At about ten-thirty, Linda and I said our thanks, good-byes and congratulations, and left for home. Because it had been raining throughout the day and was threatening to do so again, we had driven to Don's house, so it only took a couple minutes to get home, let the dog out one last time for the evening, set up the coffee for the next morning, and get ready for bed.

By about 10:45 p.m. I was ready for bed, lying in my pyjamas and reading a book. Linda was brushing her teeth, I think, or washing her face. It was then that the phone rang.

Now at 10:45, there are not too many reasons for the phone to ring, most of them bad. Something has happened to my mother or father. My brother or sister have been rushed to the hospital. A nephew or niece has fallen very ill. That's about it. I reached across the bed for the phone, preparing myself for bad news.

"Dave? This is Deb from next-door. I'm sorry to call so late, but Dave Black from up the street just called to tell me that he was walking his dog and he noticed that Kyle left his car window down. You and Linda are the only ones with keys to the house, so could you please get the keys and roll up the window?"

She then began to tell me where I'd find the keys, but I wasn't listening to that. Here's what I was thinking: *Mom and Dad are okay. Nothing bad has happened. Oh yeah, Ken and Deb are gone this weekend up north. Kyle left the window down? His seat will be soaked. I have to roll the window up, but I'm in my pyjamas. Should I get dressed again? Just put on a bathrobe? Socks? No, just shoes—*

"No problem, Deb, I'm happy to take care of that."

"Thanks Dave. I owe you one."

"Nope: last month you watered our plants and brought in the mail when we were away. This is the least I can do."

I hung up the phone, put on my bath robe and my shoes, found the keys for Ken and Deb's house, and went next door. Linda told me that the keys probably opened the side door, not the front. She was right.

I had no problem opening the door, but the house was in complete darkness. I felt for the light switch, but there wasn't one by the door. There are four or five steps up from the doorway to Ken's kitchen. I walked up them very slowly in the darkness, and then found out that there was a glass door at the top of the stairs by bumping my nose against it.

I opened that door and felt around on the wall for the light switch, but there wasn't one there, either. My eyes must have been getting used to the dark, because I could just make out the switches on the opposing wall. I switched on the lights and then saw the reason I told you you needed to know Ken was a car guy: on a series of hooks were the keys for all of Ken's cars, Deb's car, Kyle's car, Paige's car, and what-all else. I stared at them for a minute, coming to the realization that they were all Chrysler car keys. The fobs and the keys themselves all looked remarkably similar. *I wonder how they tell them apart each morning?* I thought.

I grabbed them all off the hooks and went back outside, stuffing most of them into my bathrobe pockets. I went across the street to Kyle's car and saw that, yes, my neighbour Dave was right, Kyle had left the passenger side window down. I took the first set of keys and pressed the unlock button. Nothing happened. I pressed the lock button and nothing happened again. I put that key in my right bathrobe pocket.

I repeated the process with the next three sets, with the same results. When I got to the fourth set, I unlocked Deb's car in the driveway, and turned on her lights. Because I was beginning to get frustrated, I pressed her panic button, for just a second, and ensured that this set was not going to help me.

I worked my way through all the keys I had brought outside, and had only one key left—a simple metal key with no plastic fob, and no buttons to press. I slid it into the door handle, noting how smoothly it went in, and was surprised when it wouldn't turn.

I took it out and tried again. Same result.

I jiggled the key. Still wouldn't turn.

Now I started thinking. Maybe Kyle is more like me than Ken. Maybe he's not much of a car guy and this, his first car, was, like my first car, a crap car. Maybe if I get in the passenger side door, this key will slide into the ignition and I'll be able roll the window up and get back to bed.

I went around to the passenger side, tried the door and wasn't surprised to find it locked. I reached in through the window, unlocked the door, opened it and—

AHNNN!—AHNNN!—AHNNN!—AHNNN!—AHNNN!

I'd set off the car alarm! Shit!

AHNNN!—AHNNN!—AHNNN!—AHNNN!—AHNNN!

I closed the door and ran back to the house.

AHNNN!—AHNNN!—AHNNN!—AHNNN!—AHNNN!

I raced into the kitchen, and looked at the hooks—all empty—

AHNNN!—AHNNN!—AHNNN!—AHNNN!—AHNNN!

Shit! Umm, where else might there be keys?

AHNNN!—AHNNN!—AHNNN!—AHNNN!—AHNNN!

I wondered how long the alarm would go before the battery died. I wondered how long it would be until the police arrived. I knew that I was waking up the whole neighbourhood. Shit! There! On the kitchen table, one set of keys I'd missed! In the back of my brain, I heard Deb saying, "Kyle's keys are on the table by the window closest to Gino's house." They were on a plastic running shoe key fob, or a soccer ball thing—something a twenty-two year old kid who leaves his window down on a day it was going to rain and he was going away for the weekend would own—

AHNNN!—AHNNN!—AHNNN!—AHNNN!—AHNNN!

I picked them up and ran back out to the car, pressing the panic button as I ran, but the car alarm just got faster—AHNNN!—AHNNN!—AHNNN!—AHNNN!—AHNNN!

I unlocked the door, got in and looked at the dashboard. I noticed, with concern, that there wasn't a key hole or an ignition switch. Shit! I looked at the key fob and noticed with even more concern that there wasn't even a key! Shit! I began pressing buttons. I opened the trunk. I locked the doors and unlocked them again. Shit! I read the message on the dashboard—

AHNNN!—AHNNN!—AHNNN!—AHNNN!—AHNNN!

I read the message on the dashboard.

"To start the car, press on the brake and push the start button."

Can't hurt. I followed the instructions—"AHNNN—" The car started, and the alarm stopped.

I rolled up the window. Figured out how to stop the car and then started laughing.

There was a knock on the window. I looked up, expecting the police, "Sorry for the trouble officer. You see—" It was Ginny from across the street, my seventy-something-year-old neighbour with the barking Yorkies. She had a flashlight and a telephone. She was saying something, but I couldn't make it out through the closed window.

I got out of the car, still laughing.

"Oh, it's you! Do you have Deb's phone number?"

"Why do you want to call Deb? She and Ken are up north."

"Oh. Well, Kyle's window is down…"

"No it's not. I just put it up, and you just knocked on it. You didn't just call the police, did you?"

"Well, no, not yet, but I was just coming out to see who was making all the commotion, and was getting set to…"

I don't really think she thought I was trying to steal Kyle's car in my pyjamas and bathrobe, but I noticed that she didn't turn her phone off until I'd just about finished telling her my story. I said good-night to her, both of us still laughing, and I started walking towards Ken and Deb's house.

"Hey Dave?"

"Yes?"

"Do you think we should close Kyle's trunk?"

Now the only thing that would make this story perfect would be if I'd accidentally locked myself out of my house, which I had. Fortunately, Linda hadn't gone to sleep, and she let in a sheepish, but laughing, husband.

What of the nice neighbourhood I live in? Why hadn't anyone come to help me?

Dan, who lives right across the street, had left to pick up his daughter, just as my episode began. "I wonder why Dave's out in his bathrobe?" he thought to himself as he drove away.

And Dave Black, who lives up the street and who had started the whole thing by calling Deb way up north to let her know about her son's car window, was just drifting off to sleep when the car alarm went off. His wife, Sandra, looked out her bedroom window and saw me racing across the lawn in my bathrobe to get the last set of keys.

"Uh, Dave? Dave Garlick's running across Ken's lawn and Kyle's alarm is going off. Do you think you should go help him?"

From a thousand miles away, and very near sleep, Dave responded, "It's Garlick? Everything's okay. He's got this . . ."

Printed in Canada